LIGHT ON
DISTANT HILLS

LIGHT ON
DISTANT HILLS

A Memoir

CATHAL O'SEARCAIGH

SIMON &
SCHUSTER

London · New York · Sydney · Toronto
A CBS COMPANY

First published in Great Britain by Simon & Schuster UK Ltd, 2009
A CBS COMPANY

1 3 5 7 9 10 8 6 4 2

Simon & Schuster UK Ltd
1st Floor
222 Gray's Inn Road
London WC1X 8HB

www.simonandschuster.co.uk

Simon & Schuster Australia
Sydney

A CIP catalogue record for this book is available
from the British Library.

ISBN: 978-1-84737-063-1

Typeset by M Rules

Printed in the UK by CPI Mackays, Chatham ME5 8TD

For Prashant

AUTHOR'S NOTE

This memoir is set in a Gaelic-speaking community but from the start I decided that I wasn't going to have the people who inhabit these pages speaking in translation. I feared, if I took up that option, rendering it into some kind of English passing-off as Gaelic, that the dialogue would be self-consciously mannered. In fact, the solution was simpler than trying to grapple with the vexed complexities of translation. Instead I used the idiomatic, everyday English that is spoken in Donegal with its characteristic whimsy and its Gaelic turn of phrase. This register, not only enriched as it is by borrowings from Gaelic, but shaped by its speech patterns, is, I feel, a better choice, and more natural than a contrived translation.

PROLOGUE

Writing this memoir, I was reminded of Melquíades, the gypsy in Gabriel García Márquez's *One Hundred Years of Solitude* who with two powerful magnets goes around the village of Macando plucking out from secret nooks things which people had misplaced and were searching for in vain – the metallic hoardings of a neighbourhood – lost in hidden crannies. 'Things have a life of their own. It's simply a matter of waking up their souls,' the gypsy says, explaining his rare gift of retrieval.

I became that gypsy, writing this memoir, in that I was pulling out things which I had lost, mislaid or hidden away in the crevices of my memory. In retrieving the past one is trying to make a presence of an absence, a task more hazardous, I dare say, than finding screws and nails in secret nooks.

Evoking a lost domain of emotions and experiences requires one to be a fabulist and a conjurer. In that sense, this memoir is both a confession and a fictional artifice. 'Experience', that raw entity, is never enough. One has to shape it; select, arrange and recreate it. That requires art as well as authenticity.

Mín A Leá, meaning 'the plain of the flagstones', where this story is mostly set, lies in the hills four miles above the village of Gortahork in North West Donegal. Mount Errigal looms in the background, an upthrust of glinting grey. Sometimes it can be imperially male in a grey suit of rain, at other times it can be endearingly homely in a brown homespun of heather. I like to think of it as a witnessing presence in our lives. My people have survived here for many generations, small hill farmers, struggling but singing. '*Tiocfaidh críoch ar an tsaol*,' they would say, '*ach mairfidh ceol agus gaol.*' The world will end but love and music will go on forever.

Creativity for me arises out of my deep attachment to this place, out of a reverential affection for its people. My poems are devotional in the sense that they are prayerful celebrations of place, tongue and tradition. My work has become known because of its connectedness with this place. I have become a collector of its oral traditions, an archivist of its memories and its myths, a guardian of its Gaelic. This is, I suppose, a political act, acknowledging the local, recording and registering what is past or passing. In our time, the tidal wave of Anglo-American culture with its fast foods, its disposable beliefs, its throwaway morality is sweeping over indigenous customs everywhere and drowning out local ways of life. Our communities, as Joseph Campbell so aptly observed, no longer have 'controlled horizons'.

This is a memoir about growing up in the fifties and sixties on a Donegal hill farm. It's about coming of age in a tight-knit community with its rustic domesticity, its seasonal routines, its ritualistic lifestyle. It's about a cast of characters who coloured my childhood: keepers of knowledge, dispensers of folk wisdom, storytellers who handed down an incomparable oral tradition of ancestral lore. And, above all, it's about a child who marvels at what is happening to him as he grows up in that locale, which is both a parish of the past and a place in the present.

The book ends with an account of a short, liberating spell in London. While there I had a defining moment and it became clear to me that Gaelic was to be my literary language. The muse of poetry beckoned. She connected me to the vital creative energies of my *dúchas* and charmed me back home.

I wish for this – although one never knows with a piece of writing what fate awaits it once it hits the shelves – that it has a rich immediacy about it, an earthy, commonsense mysticism that will allow it to go beyond its local geography. *Beir beannacht.*

PART ONE

It takes little talent to see clearly what lies under one's nose, a good deal of it to know in which direction to point that organ.

W.H. Auden

I'm sitting on the bare flagstoned floor of our kitchen at Mín A Leá wearing a coarse, woollen gansey and a pleated wrap-around tartan skirt secured at the side by a big shiny safety pin. It's 1955 and my mother keeps telling me that I'm three years old and big enough now to be wearing short trousers instead of a skirt. There is a dangle of snot hanging from my nostrils which slithers in and out as I breathe like a green tapered grub. I must have been bawling for attention because she throws me a book to quiet me down. She has discovered that a book from the stack on the dresser can distract me when I'm bothersome and wheedle me into the best of humour.

I find this chunky wedge of paper irresistible – its soft leafy sheen, the spiky jottings stretched like lines of barbed wire across each page – but more than anything else it is its smell that attracts me. It reminds me of the strong, heady smell that I inhale off the trunk in the bedroom when occasionally its curved, hinged lid is lifted. It is where the family papers and the money is kept, the tea set and the linen that my grandmother gave us, and Mother's jewellery set; her brooches, a few white, beady necklaces and one glittery ring. It is always locked and Mother becomes cross if I pester her to open it.

The smell reminds me as well of snug corners around the house where I curl up now and then to be on my own, and the dark cubbyholes where I've found wondrous things: old chalky-white pipes, glitzy bits of delph, rusty nails. It is the smell of secrets and I am intrigued by it.

When I had slavered over the book for a while, thumbing through it and smelling it, I began to pull it apart. The pages came away easily in my hand. I gripped each one and squeezed it into a tight ball, hoping to wring out all those curious smells that pleasured me. My father appeared in the doorway, his thumb latched in his brown galluses, a pained look on his face when he saw his book littered over the floor.

'Why did you give him my book, Agnes?' he admonishes my mother softly.

'It's just an ould book, Micky,' my mother says scornfully, her words sharp as the bright knives on the table which she will not allow me to handle or play with. I sit there, vaguely absorbed in the book and at the same time watching how upset my father is at the mess I've made of it. My mother stands at the table in her blue polka-dot apron staring at my father, a stubborn look on her face.

'A book is the only way to calm that child,' she says impatiently.

'There's no good talking to you,' my father says timidly, almost apologetically. He bends down, gathers the torn pages together and tries to sort them out. I know that he's put out by what I have done, but why I can't grasp. I want to snuggle up to him and breathe in the hot whiff of cow byre that I always get off his clothes.

'Good book, Daddy,' I say, looking up at him encouragingly. He smiles, picks me up in his arms and cleans my snotty nose with the rough cuff of his plaid shirt.

'It was good 'til you got your hand on it, *a chroí*.'

His voice is as soft as the sweet, blobby blackberries that he picked for me the evening before when I went with him to fetch Suckie Mhór, our cow, from the field by the river.

'You should heed the books, *a thaisce*, they'll be there when you're able to read. They'll be like a small door for you into a big world.'

4

It's a winter's night. A draught sweeps up the floor and makes the turf fire cackle and wheeze like a clucking hen. Hot sparks chirp like wee chicks and flutter up the chimney. I'm sitting on a creepie, a child's stool, imagining that the cackling flames are a hen's roost. Having no one to play with, I amuse myself with these flights of fancy.

Granda, my daddy's father who lives with us, is gone off to a wake in Dunlewey. He's a great sport and doesn't mind at all playing with me. When he's about, he keeps me on the go with his games. My favourite one is called *Cuartaigh*, Search. While I have my face to the wall, he hides something behind my back, a comb, a shoe, a cup, and then I have to find it. We also play cards, snap and donkey and twenty-five. And he asks me riddles, puzzles me terribly with the match tricks and has me laughing my head off with his Paddy the Irishman jokes. He has a story, I think, about every person and every place in the parish. He also tells me that I'm related to this family and that family and it seems to be that I'm connected to everybody in the place, not only those who are living but also those who are dead.

'All them dead wans! Aye boy, there's a power of the past in yer blood,' he's fond of saying. If all of them that came before me are in my blood, I must be as old as the hills. It was a scary thought. I mentioned it to Granda.

'Am I very old, Granda?'

'What puts a question like that on yer tongue, *a leanbh*?'

'If all of them old wans are living in me blood,' I said, 'I must be nearly as old as you.'

'For a four-year-old child, ye surely have an old head on ye.'
And he laughed and seemed pleased. 'But to answer your
question, aye, I suppose you belong to them as much as you
belong to me.' If they were all as good as Granda, I didn't really
mind belonging to them.

I also like to link things together, find association. Something
clicks in my head when I find an apt connection between one
thing and another, a bright light is switched on inside my
forehead and I forget myself. Poems are very good at coupling
things together, making startling connections.

> First came the primrose
> On the bank high
> Like a maiden looking forth
> From the window of a tower
> When the battle rolls below
> So looked she
> And saw the storms go by.

My father likes this poem and often reads it to me. It's called 'A
Chanted Calendar'. I like it myself, because it's about the wild
flowers that I know; the primrose, the daisy and the cowslip. In a
poem, the words seem to swirl along on some strong current like
the wild flowers I sometimes drop into the stream below the house
and watch as they drift away in the steady flow. My father says that
there is a link between everything but only some people can see
these secret links. 'Poets' he calls those people who are good at
seeing the hidden connections. When I think of one thing and
equate it with another thing, maybe I'm also making a poem.

My mother's at the table mixing boiled potatoes and flour. She
kneads and pounds the mixture into a large, flat slab which she
then spreads out on the griddle and places on the open fire to

cook. This is fadge, and we will have it later for supper. My father comes in from the byre where he's been keeping an eye on an ailing heifer. 'How's she doing?' my mother asks him anxiously.

'She's on the mend, thanks be to God. That chemist's dose did the job.'

My father looks relieved. He sits by the fireside and pulls out a pipe from the inside pocket of his jacket. It's the small one with the chunky bowl and a curl on the stem. He strikes a match and lights it up. Then he gives it a few quick drags until it gasps and reddens into life with a flicker of sparks. He puffs away at it, fragrant smoke rising like a flurry of pot-bellied angels in flight about his head.

'Daddy, will you say a poem?' I ask him when I know that he has puffed enough of it and is ready to talk.

'I will indeed, *a chroí*. What one d'ye want to hear?'

'The one about the mouse,' I say eagerly.

'You're the devil for Robbie Burns, aren't you?'

He leans forward, cups his chin in a big calloused palm, closes his eyes and begins to recite. As he says it, his body begins to sway back and forth, slowly, like the press and pull of a melodeon. His voice, too, has the same slow hum and sigh of a melodeon when someone plays a sad tune on it. I'm drawn into this low, mournful croon and I sit there gripped by the hushed power of it. Although I don't understand all the words in the poem, I know the story and feel tears welling up in my eyes for the little mouse whose winter house was run through by the plough. When he finishes, he draws his chair up close to the chimney corner. He spreads out his palms and warms them over the hot glow of the fire. Ash flakes swirl up around his hands like the fluffy down of newborn chicks. 'All his life, Robbie Burns was stuck in the trap of poverty,' he says in a broody voice, peering over at me.

'Like us, Daddy.'

'Aye. But things will get better.'

'When?'

'When? If I knew that, son, I'd be a rich fortune-teller.'

Mother hands each of us a big mug of steaming tea and places a plate of hot, buttered fadge on the hearth. We sit in silence, sipping at our scalding tea and munching the tasty potato treats that drip with butter.

'Aye, indeed, Robbie *bocht* had his fill of ups and downs,' my father says, more to himself than to me. I know exactly what he means because he has often told me about Robbie's life as a failed farmer, but I want to cheer him up.

'Was he on a seesaw, Daddy?' I say innocently.

He laughs at that. For a big, brawny man his laugh is soft and girlish. It has a tinkling sound as if little tinny bells are going ding-dong in it. Bluebells would chime like that, I imagined, if they could jingle their bells. My father's laugh is soothing and I want him to laugh all the time.

'You're some laddie buck, so you are.' He grabs hold of me and puts me sitting on his lap.

'Daddy, I heard a man in Niall Rua's shop say that money talks,' I tell him. A broad grin spreads across his soft face the way sunshine sometimes lights up the brow of a hill.

'It only talks, son, when you have heaps of it. Then it has plenty of ould gab.'

'It doesn't talk at all in my piggy bank.'

'You have too much rattle in your wee bank, that's why. It's the pounds that talk, *a chroí*, not the pennies.'

I see a mouse scoot across the floor and disappear behind the dresser. It came into the house from an adjoining byre where we store hay and straw, knobbly sacks of potatoes and soft, swelled-up bags of oats. I'm still thinking about the mouse in the poem having to face the cold, sleety winter without its snug little nest.

'Daddy, I'll never kill a mouse.' He finds this highly amusing and chuckles away to himself.

'I'll blame Robbie Burns if you end up with a rooky house crawling with mice.'

Our own house is small. The kitchen, where we spend most of the time, has a corner bed in it for Granda and below that a wee pantry with a door into it. The room where Mammy and Daddy have their bed is brightly whitewashed and always appears to be smiling. Some nights I sleep with Granda, other nights with my parents. We have an outside lavatory which my father built on top of the stream that runs down through our farm and washes out into the river. Everyone else in Mín A Leá has a dry lavatory but we have running water in ours. The neighbours think it's very clever and they compliment my father for coming up with such a practical idea.

'You wouldn't get any better in America,' my granda is fond of saying whenever somebody praises my father's handiwork. It's a very calming place and the neighbours use it regularly. The flowing water, it seems, helps people to relax when they are relieving themselves. Word has got out that it's a good place to relieve constipation and occasionally somebody comes to try it out for themselves. However, it makes me nervous because I imagine that the water is a group of giddy, tittering girls watching me with my trousers down.

'Don't let that child out of your sight,' my mother said as she slicked back my hair with a lick of spit. Granda cocked his head to one side and looked at her with a twinkle in his eye.

'That bucko, he'll be keeping the eye on me,' he said, and laughed. He was standing in front of the cracked mirror that hung on a nail by the window, fastening the neck of his shirt with a tiny gilt stud that looked like an eye. Whenever he wore it I felt it was watching me.

Granda had one good jacket, a brownish tweed that he wore to Mass, to funerals and to fairs. He put it on and pulled a rumpled check cap over his bald, shiny head.

'Right, me bucko, we're ready for the road,' he said, nudging me out the door. I kissed my mother quickly and swaggered out after him, full of myself. I was five years old and wearing my first long trousers, a pair of black cords that Auntie Biddy sent from Glasgow, and Granda was taking me to the August fair in Falcarragh.

'I'm warnin' you, Joe, don't be a buck eejit with your money and for God's sake don't go on the randan,' my mother yelled at him as we walked through a mucky gap at the cow byre.

'As much as would drown a wren, Agnes, I won't let past me mouth,' he called and then gave her a big salute with his cap. I saw him lick the tip of his grey moustache the way he did when he sipped a wee nip of whiskey by the fireside and I knew he had no intention of keeping that promise. My mother always gave him 'a good scowl' when he came home drunk, which meant she ate the head off him. They'd 'have words' as she put it, snarling at each other like cross dogs. When Granda couldn't stand it any longer he'd stumble off to the barn and, for an hour or two, sleep it off in the straw. By then, Mother would have calmed down. She'd bring him in to the fire, feed him and fuss over him.

We took the grassy path through the fields down to the river.

'Do ye see that harvest?' Granda said, admiring our two fields of ripening corn.

'She be kinda good this year.'

A breeze rippled the stalks so that they nodded their grainy heads as if agreeing with what Granda said.

'Look at that now,' he said, watching the swaying corn with pleasure.

'We're blessed to be alive.'

We crossed the river on the round, wobbly stones that looked like Granda's worn-down, yellowed back teeth. I saw a trout flash and wiggle out of sight. A quick tongue of water gurgled around the stones like the soft, licking sounds I made after eating something sweet. I was looking forward to the thick stick of pink and white rock that Granda promised to buy me at the fair.

We walked through a bit of sedgy bog and came out onto the road at Mullaney's farm. Dan Mullaney was making a start at the harvest. His bright-edged scythe glinted like a fish among tumbling swathes of corn.

'She's a grand day for cutting,' Granda shouted across to him.

'Aye boy, she's wild dry, so she is,' Dan said, without straightening up. Stooped forward slightly and with a slow unhurried stroke of the scythe, he cut the corn in wide sweeping curves

It was a hot still morning, a low-lying light hugged the hills and they sprawled out like cows at ease in the sun. They seemed so near I could almost stroke their craggy foreheads. I was so happy I wanted to hold the soft, dozy morning in my arms like a small puppy. Even though it was mostly uphill I bounced along in front of my granda as springy as if I were getting a ride on a piled-up cart of hay.

At the top of the brae we took a breather while Granda lit up his pipe. It was so calm he didn't have to shield the match with his hands when he struck it. In the hush we could hear the rattle of a horse cart and the jingle of a harness somewhere further down the glen. I could see my mother hanging out the washing below the house. Mín A Leá, on the other side of the glen, looked so homely and cosy, its sloping fields of green and gold spread out like a bed of sheets drying in the sun. A moorhen cackled across the bog and settled on a small, lit-up hill. It was slanted to one side like the cocky way that cattle dealers sometimes wore their hats.

'Granda, what's the name of that shiny hill over there?'

He had a name for every bit of the land. I liked those names and the stories that went with them. If you knew their names, a field, a hill, a bog, a rock became friendlier and easier to get along with Granda told me.

'They call that the Cnoc Breac, *a chroí*, the speckled hill.'

'Why?'

'I'm not rightly sure but if you look at it, see, it has a wild streak of browns in it like my cap.'

I could see the browns alright; some were the colour of rusting tin cans, and others were more coppery like nuts at Hallowe'en. Granda sucked his pipe and it gurgled like a baby cooing.

'That's Ard na mBothóg down there at the turn of the road, the hill of the huts,' he said, pointing to a stony rise by the roadside.

'In the old days people used to be living there in wee sod houses, that's how it came by that name.' He shuffled about a bit, gazed into the distance and when he spoke his voice was low and serious.

'I saw meself lights there one night when I was coming home late from the cards. Wee flutters of light they were, the likes of I never seen. I didn't ask what they were, for I knew rightly they weren't of this world. Says I to meself, I better be making tracks and I ran like the bejasus for fear they'd take a hault of me. I'll tell ye I was out in some cold sweat when I got home.'

I could see him twitch his shoulders and shiver. He then puffed furiously at his pipe as if he needed something to warm himself up. Big shadows flitted across the faraway mountains like skeletons and were gone. I knew from my mother and from my granda that the bones of the past often came alive and wandered into the present. I didn't want to think about that because it frightened me, so I looked at the loveliness around me. Thistles with their bright buttons of purple grew alongside the road and when I glanced across the glen I saw a purple glow rise off the ridge of heather above our house. I took Granda's hand and we dandered up the road to the bus.

At the bus stop a cluster of women in bright headscarves and coloured dresses stood chatting. Behind them, men in open-necked shirts and caps sat on a rushy bank smoking their pipes.

'That's a mighty day, Joe,' one of the men said, as we crossed the road to join the waiting crowd.

'You couldn't beat it with a stick,' Granda said, in a loud jolly voice, and they all laughed.

I swanked around and showed off my new long trousers. A small, grey-haired woman with lines in her face like cracks inside a cup came over and patted me on the back.

'The wee fella is a big man now, Joe, with the long trousers on him.' I was pleased that she noticed them.

'Aye, he'll be chasing the lassies in no time at all, Mary.'

She took a dim view of that, I think, because her face broke into a severe scowl. I thought it would crack open.

'He'd do a nice wee priest, God bless him, if youse keep him at the books.'

'If we could make a living ourselves, Mary, maybe we could make a priest out of him,' Granda said, and gave her a roguish smile. Then he cleared his throat and spat out a big glob of spit. It landed in a trickle of water beside the road and floated like frothy suds. I was watching it drift away when one of the women shouted, 'She's coming up the brae!' I listened and heard the clanky drone of the bus as it heaved its way uphill through the bog. Then it rattled around a bend, a sudden whiteness, and came to a shuddering halt where we stood. There was a lot of friendly jostling and laughter as we pressed into the bus. Manus Rua, the conductor, stood by the doorway and greeted everybody by name as they came aboard.

'How's the auld buck himself today?' he asked Granda as we stepped up into the bus.

'If I was any better than I am, I wouldn't recognise meself,' Granda said, and handed him the fare.

'That's a good complaint, Joe,' Manus Rua said. He clicked and punched the tickets and rattled the black, scuffed moneybag that hung low at his side out of which he poked loose change and handed it back to Granda, along with the tickets.

The engine spluttered, the bus shook and we were off in a belch of bluish smoke down the road. Granda and I staggered to a back seat. I sat on the inside, put my nose to the window and watched the countryside drift by as if it were going in the opposite direction. I saw a house on the edge of the bog suddenly brighten up, whitewashed in light, and then darken again. I saw a blue and red cart heeled up by the roadside and an old man swabbing it down with a big bushy heather broom. Harvesters out in the fields straightened up and waved when the bus passed. I waved back at them. Here and there we slowed to a halt and another heave of passengers came aboard. Soon we were sitting three and four to a seat and many had to stand, but they didn't seem to mind. Granda was lively company and made everyone around him happy with his funny sayings. People liked him because he made them smile. I was glad that he was my granda and when a man with sleek black hair who sat beside us said, 'I declare to God, the wee fella is the spit of yourself, Joe,' I was overjoyed. I wanted to be like Granda and put people in good spirits with a word and a smile. Somewhere near Gortahork the bus rounded a corner and tilted steeply to one side. I thought it was going to topple over and I clung tightly to Granda. He steadied himself by gripping the seat in front of him.

'Keep her on the road, Johnny, or we'll all be kilt dead,' he roared up at the driver and everybody cheered.

'We'll be there in a few minutes,' he told me as we rattled out of Gortahork and he grinned and sucked his draggly moustache. The sea, a green-blue shininess, tumbled about and rolled into Killult Bay to our left.

When I told him that it was a ghost trapped inside a green bottle, he laughed and said, 'You're a wild man for the fancy ideas.' Soon we creaked our way up a big brae and into Falcarragh.

Out in the street the air was moist with the hot reek of animals. Like a damp rag smack in my face, it took my breath away. I held on to Granda's hand as we squeezed our way up the thronged footpath. Being close to him bolstered me up. He stopped here and there to have a passing word with people that he knew. A lot of them spoke in English and I didn't understand what they were saying. When Granda spoke in English his voice sounded creaky, like a rusty gate squeaking in the wind. He wasn't at ease in it.

I knew this from the way he scraped out the words as if he found it hard to get hold of them. When he spoke in Gaelic his voice was warm and I felt closer to him.

One side of the street was lined with stalls. Big bundles of clothes lay heaped on trestle tables under tarpaulin coverings. A thin man with small pudgy hands and a ring of flaky dandruff around his collar sold men's working clothes: corduroy trousers, flannel shirts, cloth caps and soiled jackets. He was doing good business. People crowded around his stall, held up the clothes to the light, rubbed and sniffed them and haggled over the price. He and Granda blathered away in English. I didn't understand what they were saying so I tugged at Granda's sleeve and asked.

'Why are you talking in English?'

He scratched his head and spoke softly as if whispering.

'We'll have to talk in English, *a chroí*, or the townies here'll think we're from the bog.'

I wasn't sure whether he was serious or just taking a hand at me. Granda was always carrying on and codding me about things. I couldn't make sense of what he was saying. Why did we have to keep quiet about where we came from and why was he making a connection between the bog and what we spoke?

'But aren't we from the bog, Granda?' I asked him out loud and it was met with a burst of laughter from those gathered around the stall. I felt everybody was looking at me. A hot flush of shyness came to my cheeks. A man who was trying on an old patched jacket with specks of green and blue in it looked up and said, 'We're up to our bloody arse in bog, so we are. That's why you'll have to learn English for it to be drained out of you.'

He sounded angry. I watched him fling the jacket back on the heaped pile of clothes as if it were worthless. His eyes were steely grey like nails. When he turned towards me I got stuck to them and couldn't budge. I stood there staring at him.

'If you want to get ahead in the world you'll have to have English.' He spoke sharply. 'Gaelic won't take you beyond Gortahork.' I know that he wasn't just talking to me. He was addressing the whole lot of us gathered around the stall.

'He's as sharp as a stab, that scoundrel. Always giving off about Gaelic,' said a woman with a broad face and pins in her hair when he moved off down the street.

'Is Gaelic no good, Granda?' I asked him anxiously. All this talk left me puzzled.

He took my small hand in his knobbly palms and squeezed it gently.

'I wouldn't say it's no good but it's better when you have a bit of English to back it up.'

The woman with the broad face handed me a sweet with a green shiny wrapper on it.

'A wee caramel to keep you munchin',' she said. 'Where's your tongue? Stick it out 'til I see it.'

She was kind and I wanted to please her.

'It's curled up like a wee purse,' she said, studying my tongue. 'I bet you have a big stash of English words hidden away in there.'

A purse for words. I thought about that as we dawdled up the street. I tried to count all the English words I had, but got muddled up by the din around me and lost count after twenty. It was nice to think of words as things you kept in a purse like money. 'Mother', I thought, made a crinkly sound like a new pound note and a word like '*lá aonaigh*', fair day, jingled like a coin. I was beginning to think that English words had more value to them than Gaelic words.

Granda doted on me and we chatted away in Gaelic as we strolled through the fair. A grey tractor trundled down the street with a truckload of sheep. Pigs in a box bedded with straw grunted and squealed. We made our way up to an open area by the roadside where cattle and sheep were sold. The ground was glossy with the green slush of their shite. In a weedy corner under trees two men were haggling over a brown cow. The one who held her on a slack rope said, 'Look at the two bellies on that cow. Mind you, she's a decent beast even if it's meself that says it.' Tall dusty nettles with hairy stems grew nearby. The cow curled a long, probing tongue around the leaves and nipped them cautiously. I wondered how the cow could do that without getting stung. The other man leaned on his stick and guffawed.

'Man dear, she's full of wind. You'd catch a cowld if she farted.'

He whacked her on the rump with the flat of his hand. Without warning the cow gave a brisk swing of her tail, lashed him across the arm and knocked the stick out of his hand. I hid behind Granda and giggled. The man picked up his stick and, muttering to himself, walked away, a scabby dog yelping at his heels.

'Be raisonable and give me a decent price,' the owner of the cow shouted after him.

'If I got her for nothing I'd not be having that dunty cow,' he spat back at him.

'Are you going to make a bid yerself?' the owner said, noticing me. I fingered the shilling I had in my trouser pocket and remained silent.

There was a lot of slapping of shoulders and spitting on palms going on as people clenched deals and handed over 'lucky money'. A huddle of scrawny calves tethered to a gate looked sad and kept bobbing their heads and fluttering their long, pale eyelashes. A black one with a white spot in the middle of its forehead nuzzled up to me and licked my fingers with a soft, furry tongue. Then I thought about the stick of rock.

'Granda, can we buy the rock now?'

'Aye, surely.'

We went into Charlie Greene's, a busy grocery store with a timber counter running the length of it. A big slicer with a fat roll of bacon gleamed on the counter. Tin buckets and shiny kettles hung from the ceiling. Puffy cakes with white icing, scones stuffed with cream and crumbly buns with raisins were stacked in a glass bin. A rich aroma of smells filled the shop; tea, snuff, fresh bread, soap. A small bulky woman in a black fringed shawl and a coarse black skirt, who was talking to herself, was being served. When I coughed behind her she turned around and wagged a finger at me. I got a strong sniff of drink off her heavy breath, but I let on that I didn't see her and watched the shop boy scoop out sugar from a heavy sack, weigh it on white enamel scales using round brass measures, the needle flicking to and fro like a pecking bird until it stopped at the exact weight.

Next he took down a tall glass jar full of brandy balls, made a funnel out of newspaper and filled it up with sticky sweets.

'Will that be all, Kitty?' he asked her politely.

'Isn't that enough?' she shrieked at him. 'If I was silly enough you'd have me fork out my last penny, you greedy git.' She took coins out of a tiny leather purse with a silver catch on it, peered at each one grudgingly as if unwilling to let it go and then rattled them one by one on the counter. The shop boy looked nervous and kept cracking the joints of his long, bony fingers while she counted out the money. When she finished he gathered up the loose change and put it into a drawer behind the counter. She shoved her goods into a small, round wicker basket and, as she was leaving, she glared at me furiously. The whites of her eyes had a yellow streak like a tobacco stain and it made her look mean and spiteful.

'She's like a kettle on the boil, that Kitty,' Granda said to me when she left the shop.

'Aye boy, when she gets a wee dram she lets off a bit of steam.'

Right enough, with her black clothes, her stoutness, her long strupy nose she did look like a sooty kettle. Thinking of her as a kettle made her seem more agreeable to me. I liked kettles because they were plump and pleasant and had a cosy, cuddly warmth about them.

'What can I do for you, Joe?' the shop boy said, smiling fondly at Granda and giving me a nod and a wink. Granda got a big fat rock in a flashy wrapper for me and a plug of tobacco for himself. Outside we sat on a sunny window ledge, and while he stoked up his pipe I sucked on my stick of rock.

I liked many kinds of sweeties – gobstoppers, lollipops, liquorice allsorts, dolly mixtures, chocolates and toffees – but the rock was my favourite. Although hard, it was deliciously luscious when I got my teeth into it. I loved the slurp and crunch of it in my mouth, the slow, sugary melt of it dribbling down my throat. Unlike a jelly baby or butterscotch that got eaten up in two bites and a gulp, a rock kept you munching pleasurably for a long time.

I knew that I would always remember this moment, the sweet suckle of rock, the throaty gulp of Granda's pipe and the two of us sitting together, touched by the sun. I knew that I would hold on to it in times to come, clasp it like a dependable hand, gaze at it like a beloved face, savour it like a soothing voice. I knew that it would become a moment of ageless tenderness and that it would still be with me, although I didn't want to dwell on this too much, when Granda would be no more.

'It's time for a wee cup of tea,' Granda said, and led me up the street and into a small café. Three men, their caps rolled up and stuck down their jacket pockets, were eating noisily at the table by the door. They looked awkward holding tiny cups in their big, rough hands. A tall, auburn-haired girl in a tight green dress and a yellow scarf bunched around her neck showed us to our table. She was as lovely in her bright colours as one of the stalks of corn we admired in our field in the morning. Granda ordered 'tea, fried eggs and a junt of bread'.

Our table was near the kitchen door and I could hear the sizzle and hiss of frying, the rattle of pans and somebody cracking eggs. It made me hungry. A woman in black with a lace veil hanging over her face sat on her own at a window table. She held pearly rosary beads laced around her fingers and between sups of tea looked up with a steadfast gaze at the white ceiling.

'What is she looking at?' I whispered into Granda's ear.

'She's lost somebody, maybe, so she's looking beyond the beyonds.'

I knew that 'lost' meant that somebody had died and 'beyond the beyonds' was Granda's name for the place that people went to when they died.

'I don't want to lose you, Granda,' I said, and touched his hand nervously. He considered this for some time, stroking his moustache.

'Man dear, there's no hurry on me to be going . . .' His voice trailed off and he shifted uneasily in his chair. I gazed at the wallpaper. It had beautiful sprawls of red and pink roses on it, so real that I could almost get their scent. Once in a book I saw a picture of heaven and it was a garden blooming with roses just like the ones on the wallpaper. God sat in a nook, a hoop of golden light above his head, his hands thrown out in a sign of welcome. As if listening, the roses were cocked towards him like ears. It didn't seem as lonely as beyond the beyonds where everybody was lost.

The waitress brought the food. Granda poured the tea, buttered a wedge of crispy white bread for me and covered it with a sludge of red jam. It was tasty so I tore into it. I found the knife and fork too tricky to use, so like Granda, I ate with my hands. When the eggs streamed and yellowed up my plate, he showed me how to dunk bread in it and soak it up. This soggy dip left yellow spills flowing down my white shirt and blue pullover.

'You have Humpty Dumpty all over you,' the waitress said, when I finished eating and she wiped it away with a wet cloth.

'Was everything alright?' she asked when Granda was settling the bill.

'You wouldn't get any better in America,' he grinned and gave her a little friendly dig in the ribs.

Outside the café, Granda got chatting to a wee stout man in a cocky hat who was buttoned into a green waistcoat that was too tight for him so that he looked like the round-bellied oil lamp that we kept as an ornament on the kitchen dresser. When he saw me looking at him he puffed out his cheeks like a globe and winked at me. I liked his round clown's face and giggled. He smiled and showed a pale rounded-off tongue like a wick.

'That's a right wee scudler you have there, Joe,' he said to Granda.

'What's your name, son?'

'Charlie.'

'That's a good one, I'm Charlie too.'

He jingled his trouser pockets, took out a handful of change and handed me a threepenny bit and a sixpence. I knew what they were because my father had taught me to recognise coins from the pictures minted on them; a hare on the threepenny bit, a hound on the sixpence. The big coppery penny had a hen and her clutch, the shilling a pig, the silver florin a salmon and the half-crown a horse. I liked the half-crown best with its silvery horse. I wanted to ride it, hear the thump of its hooves as I galloped away, a cowboy in a wide-brimmed hat, a six-shooter on my thigh and a rifle slung alongside the saddle.

'Will you have a wee drink?' Charlie asked Granda.

'A wee drink never harmed a soul,' Granda said, and he sounded pleased.

The pub was poky and dim with smoke, big blows of it drifting up to a low ceiling of black tarry rafters. The airless stink of drink made my throat dry. I followed Granda and Charlie up to the counter where a row of red-faced men sat around nodding to each other. Charlie ordered 'two bottles of stout and a slug of red lemonade for the wee man'. Granda hoisted me up by the armpits and put me sitting on a tall stool so that I could see better.

'*Sláinte,*' Charlie said, and handed me the drink. The lemonade fizzled in little frothy bubbles and made me belch out loud when I swallowed a big gulp of it too fast.

'God bless you, there's nothing like the lemonade to bring up the wind,' Granda said and patted my back.

It was exciting to be sitting in a pub with grown men. I was a wee man in long trousers, legs dangling over the stool, doing my best to look rakish. I leaned towards Charlie and Granda who were propped up against the counter and let on that I was an old hand at the gab by giving a nod and a laugh whenever I thought it was appropriate.

'Poor Johnny's gone,' Charlie said, and shook his head.

'Aye, he went fast,' Granda replied. He took a big sip of stout, smacked his lips and sucked the fringe of his moustache.

'I mind him well the last fair day standing there, the poor soul. We're blessed to be alive.'

'I heard he left a big lab behind,' Charlie said, and looked hard at Granda as if trying to sound him out.

'He was always holding on to the ha'pence,' Granda ventured cautiously.

Charlie sniffed the air and said in a narky voice, 'He wouldn't give his shite to the dogs. Look at that McFadden rabble over there,' and he gave a nod of the head towards a loud rowdy crowd sitting around a table by the far wall. 'They got it all. The whole rick-ma-tick of them are out spending it. I didn't get a penny of it and I was as near to him as any one of them.'

He pulled out a packet of Sweet Afton and proffered a cigarette to Granda. 'Man dear,' he said, 'Johnny would light up a fag in his pocket before he'd give you one.'

'My o, but he was tight,' Granda said, as he struck a match.

While they were lighting up the fags, a scuffle broke out at the McFaddens' table, a chair was overturned, somebody yelled and swore and then a balding man in wellingtons with wisps of fair straggly hair like bits of wool caught on barbed wire swayed drunkenly to the middle of the floor and shouted, 'I could buy this fuckin' town any day.' His belly sagged over his belted trousers like a small sack of wool. He swirled the drink in his glass and then tipped it into his mouth. He moved towards us, banged the glass hard on the counter, lost his footing and stumbled up against Charlie.

'Anything strange, Pat?' Charlie said casually, as if nothing had happened.

He gave Charlie a nasty look. 'Ask me arse,' he said, and staggered back to the table by the wall.

'That good-for-nothing got most of Johnny's money,' Charlie said. 'He'd drink the devil himself under the counter, so he would.'

'D'ye see that now,' Granda said, flicking ash off his fag. He ordered another round of drinks by signalling the empty glasses to the barman with a dip of his head.

'Take my tip, boy, and spend it all before you're planked and buried,' Charlie said, and smiled at me. I put my hand in my pocket and clinked my clammy one and ninepence.

A thin man with a wee pencil moustache and stubbly sideburns wearing a brown suit that was too big for him staggered to the middle of the floor and in a hoarse voice began to sing 'The Homes of Donegal'. He was getting into the swing of it and people were cocking an ear and shouting encouragements.

'Good on ye, Petey, keep it going.' Then a loud shout from the doorway stilled the place. Kitty, the rude woman we met in the shop, was storming her way through the standing crowd of drinking men.

'Give me a drag o' that fag,' she yelled and pulled the lighted cigarette out of Charlie's mouth. She crossed the floor and stood, arms crossed, glaring at the singer. I could see her grit her teeth and then she let out a growl that came from deep in her throat.

'God,' Petey gasped, 'can't you leave me alone for a wee while?'

'Wives do be wild cranky,' I heard my grandfather say.

She caught the singer by the collar of his jacket and proceeded to drag him out like an animal on a rope.

'Buck up, you good-for-nothing,' she roared at him. 'It's time you were making yourself scarce.'

Some men hooted and whistled but she gave them no heed. The barman came out and tried to shoo her away. He looked a bit nervous. He was wearing a white shirt and there were two big patches of sweat under his armpits.

'Get out of my way, ye dirty scoundrel ye,' she said and shoved him aside with a rough heave of her shoulder. 'You should be ashamed of yourself, filling this fella up with booze when ye know damn well he's a bad heart.' And off she went, pushing the singer out of the door in front of her.

'That takes the biscuit, herself comin' in and draggin' him out,' Granda said and downed his glass.

'Man alive, it's some fair day,' Charlie said and rapped the counter for more drink.

Then they started drinking wee ones.

'Damn the harm in a wee dram,' Granda said after his third whiskey. I noticed that he had a silly look on his face. He laughed a lot and licked his moustache. The tiny gilt stud on his shirt was watching me and it reminded me of a magpie's eye.

'One for sorrow,' my mother declared whenever she noticed a lone magpie lingering around our house. I knew I had to get him out of the pub.

'Granda, we'll go outside,' I pleaded with him.

'What's the hurry on you?' he spoke as if the words were slippy and he couldn't get his tongue around them.

'Here, a wee sip of stout,' and he lifted the glass to my mouth with a shaky hand. It tasted sour and musty like the inside of our henhouse. I coughed and spewed it out all over my new black trousers.

'My o, they're well blessed now,' he said, chuckling away to himself. His glass shook and creamy blobs dribbled over his fingers like rosary beads. I was anxious about him but I couldn't get him to leave. Wasn't my mother always telling him, 'mark my words, the drink'll be the death of you.'

A man with spiky red hair sat snoring on a chair by the counter. He had pockmarks all over his face like the woodworm in our byre door. I was getting annoyed and restless, so I started to count those pockmarks. I sat stock still and fixed my eyes on his face and tried not to let my mind wander. I was absorbed in this game when I heard a sudden thud at my back. I glanced over my shoulder and there was Granda sagging to the floor, his hand reaching out for me. I leaped off the stool and bent down beside him. He lay stretched on the floor and his eyes were round and staring like the eyes of a fish.

'Granda is dead,' I bawled out and tears streamed down my face. I looked at the gaping faces of strangers clustered around me and felt lost.

'Damn the dead,' Charlie said. He was sprinkling water on Granda's face and pushing down and pinching his chest.

'He's coming to.'

Everybody pressed forward and I was helpless in the rough crush until the man with the pockmarked face grabbed me and held me high on his shoulders. Granda was gulping for air, sucking big mouthfuls of it into himself and then swooshing it out again. He was coming across water, I thought, splashing his way back to me. One of the McFaddens was on his knees cradling his head and another man was helping him to sit up. He jerked his head a wee bit and groaned.

'Where is Charlie *beag*?' he said, and looked through watery eyes.

'Here Granda, here,' I shouted from my high perch.

His face looked a bit washed out and grey but there was a glimmer of light in his eye. I wiped the wet snivel from my face, slid off the man's shoulder and pushed my way to Granda's side. I took hold of his big heavy hand and held it to my mouth. It had the fresh breath of ripening corn and the fusty odour of a cow byre.

'Were you dead, Granda?' I asked him.

Everybody thought that was funny and they laughed.

Granda gave me a big sigh and smiled.

'Aye boy, I was nearly beyond the beyonds.'

In the evening, Charlie got a mate of his to drive us home; a man with a round, shrunken face like a dried-up apple, who sat hunched over the wheel and didn't say much. Charlie sat in the front with his elbow hanging out over the rolled-down window and sang snatches of 'The Wild Colonial Boy' in a low, groggy voice. Sometimes he'd nod off, then with a shudder he'd wake up, shake his head and say to Granda, 'Man dear, that was some fair day.'

From Gortahork upwards through Baltany and Cashelnagcorr, the cornfields on both sides of the glen gave off a pale gold light as the sun set. In the back seat, I snuggled up to Granda and held his hand. He looked frail, I thought, and a little lost. I saw an empty house by the roadside with a torn lace curtain hanging limp in the broken window. It looked sad and lonesome. Granda had the same worn-out, mournful expression in his eyes and it worried me. He asked me not to mention his 'wee fall in the pub' when we got home. I agreed, pleased to be sharing a secret with him. I was determined to keep my mouth shut because I knew that my mother would be cranky if she heard he'd collapsed in a pub.

'The two harum-scarums are back,' my mother said, greeting us at the door.

''Tis a wonder you're sober, Joe,' she said, and whistled through her teeth in amazement.

'Sober as a saint,' Granda said and slapped me gently on the back. 'The youngster here kept a good eye on me.'

'Any stir at the fair?' my father asked when he came in from the byre.

'Damn the stir,' Granda said, and gave me a sneaky little wink.

'We're blessed to be alive,' I said and winked back at him.

'You're becoming more like your grandfather every day, so you are,' my mother said as she dished out big plates of *brúitín* for our evening tea. Granda gave a drowsy yawn of contentment and pulled in to the table.

That night, sleeping with Granda in the kitchen bed, I dreamt that we were riding a white horse through a country yellow as corn. We were looking for my lost purse of words. When a grumpy old woman told us that a braddy cow had eaten it, I began to cry. Granda then gave me his own purse of words and told me to look after it while he crossed over a whiskey-coloured river to get a new one. Suddenly Granda was gone and I was alone and scared. The purse began to shake and heave and a cow with a reddish-yellow hide like a ten-shilling note dashed out of it and brayed at me in English. I woke up screaming. Granda held me close and stroked my forehead until I calmed down. When I told him what I'd seen he said, 'My o, you're a wild man for the dreams.'

Granda wasn't himself after that.

The good weather gave way to bleak, shivery days. Big damp, furry clouds lay across the hills and bogs. To me it looked as if they couldn't breathe with all the weight pressing down on them. They sagged and turned a miserable grey.

Like the weather, a change came over Granda too. He hobbled along with a stick and had difficulty breathing. Mostly he sat in front of the fire, shivered a lot and couldn't get warm, as if something icy and cold had got into him and had taken over his body. By the time the trees had lost their leaves, Granda had lost his liveliness. He took to the bed, didn't say much and rarely laughed.

'I'll not rise out again,' I heard him say to my mother one evening while she was feeding him spoonfuls of gruel by the fireside. 'The auld ticker is giving up, Agnes.'

'Go away outa that,' my mother said. 'You'll be on your feet in no time.' There was a catch in her voice as she said it and I saw her grip the back of the chair on which Granda sat. I let on to be playing with my wee toy car, wheeling it noisily around our bumpy stone floor, but I was disturbed by their talk. That night when I snuggled up to Granda to give him a goodnight hug before I went off to bed with my parents, I put my ear to his heart and heard a low, weak beat, like the slow drip that came off the roof into the rain barrel at the gable. I knew then that Granda's life was dripping away, drip by drip, and that soon he would be gone, drained out and emptied into beyond the beyonds.

Granda died on a bright, chilly night. I remember that because I went outside to get away from the commotion in the house. There was an icy nip in the air and the moon shone on the roof of the henhouse.

The glint of it, bright and sharp on the slates, reminded me of Granda's open razor, the one he sharpened so often on the long, black leather strap that hung behind the pantry door. 'The cut-throat boyo', he called it. 'If the edge is right it'll give you a shave as close to death as you'd wish to get,' he'd say to me mischievously as I watched him scrape the soapy, grey stubble off his face with a few deft flicks of the blade.

Moonlight on the roof, bright as that blade, brought home to me more forcefully than anything that was happening in the house that Granda was gone. I stood by the rain barrel at the gable and cried my eyes out. It was where Granda came for a slash at night before going to bed and the wall was streaked with a greeny scum from pissing against it. I could still get the smell of his piss and that made his absence even more unbearable. Somebody must have heard me sobbing for there was a shout, 'That child'll catch his death out there in the cold,' and they brought me in to the house.

I hardly remember anything of the wake – I was numb from the shock of it – except him lying in his coffin, a dribble of beads like black ice running through his joined hands. When I touched his stiff, dried-up face I shuddered and withdrew my hand immediately. The chill that crept into his bones in the last few months of his life had now become a deadly ice that froze up his body. All that Granda was of goodness, warmth and laughter had leaked away and in its place was this grim coldness that tried to get into my fingers when I touched it. After that I was too frightened to touch the body and kept away from the coffin.

31

Sitting by the corner bed in the kitchen where he always slept, I heard snatches of what people said about him:

'One of the best, he was . . .'

'Aye, indeed. You never said a truer word.'

'He was some man when he got going.'

'Aye, boy, he could tell you a yarn or two.'

'Joe could tell you who you were back as far as you could go.'

'Aye, surely. We're going to bury a coffin full of stories.'

'All gone, that's the pity of it. Anyway, he's up there with his own now.'

I saw my father ball up bits of the *Derry Journal* and stuff them into Granda's mouth to fill out his sagging cheeks and make him look livelier. Gagged up with paper, how could he talk to his own up there? Distressed by this thought, I took a pinch of snuff from a white saucer on the wee table by his coffin and sneezed so hard everybody thought I was choking. Secretly, I flicked a sprinkling of it above the coffin hoping that it would clear Granda's head and unblock his mouth. If I got a second chance, I promised Granda that I would pay more attention to what he was telling me.

On the day of his burial I stood by the open grave and watched four neighbours with ropes lower the coffin into the wet earth. There was a muddy puddle at the bottom of the pit and I heard the sound of sloshing water as the coffin clunked into it. A cold shiver ran through me and I pressed up against my mother for warmth. She dabbed her eyes with a hanky and sobbed quietly. My father stood beside us, head bowed, muttering prayers.

Big blowy gusts came in from the sea and the priest struggled to be heard. When he raised his voice the words that came out were as raw and screechy as the wind that howled around the headstones. It was too much for me when he raised a shovel of gravelly soil and splattered it all over the coffin; the thud and thump of it on the wood filled me with dread and I turned away and faced the hills. A short, quick burst of prayer and then the men began to fill in the grave. That was terrible until I made each shovelful of soil heaped on the coffin sound like a footstep and as the grave filled up the footsteps became fainter until I could hear them no more. Granda, I fancied, had somehow walked away from that smothering weight of earth piled on top of him.

By now it was raining hard and people were scurrying off as quick as they could. My mother was on her knees patting and stroking the wet, sticky clay with her hands as if trying to soothe it. A straggly line of bundled-up, late sympathisers waited to shake my father's hand. He stood behind my mother, his face pale and drawn, and received each in their turn. He listened to their polite words of pity and quietly thanked them for their support. Charlie, Granda's friend at the fair, was the last in the line to offer his condolences.

'Many's the time Joe and me crossed the water to Scotland and God be good to him the poor divil is going off by the water today too,' he said tearfully. He squinched up his eyes and wiped them clean with the sleeve of his black overcoat. He noticed me then and grasped my hand.

'Aye boy, we'll all have to put to sea some day, hoist the sail and leave all behind.'

He sniffled a bit and I wasn't sure whether he was weeping or laughing. I glanced at the sky and it was grey and choppy like the sea. Suddenly a cloud brightened up, white as a sail, and drifted off across the hills.

'That's Granda,' I called out enthusiastically, pointing up to the

33

gleaming cloud, but I knew from the blank looks on everybody's faces that no one saw what I was seeing. Even Charlie, who had put the thought in my mind, didn't seem to grasp that the shiny white cloud above us was a sailboat carrying off Granda.

It was September. I knew it was that time of year because the evening before while we were having tea my father said, 'You'll have to be stirring yerself up in the morning, *a chroí*, for it's September and time you were going to school. If we keep you at home any longer we'll all be in trouble.' There was a firmness in his voice that was worrying. School had been talked about before. It was hinted at when I was four, then brought up again when I was five, but nothing came of it. I didn't show any willingness to go so I thought that he had scrapped the idea altogether. Now I was six and there was an urgency in what he was saying, something that was not there before whenever the notion of going to school had been brought up. Knowing I couldn't fend it off any longer, I suggested to him that I would try it out for a day or two just to see what it was like.

'You'll have to give it a week at least,' he said, 'before you can settle in rightly.' I had no intentions of settling in, but I kept quiet about that.

'Why do I have to go to school, Daddy?' I asked him, suddenly alarmed at the terrible prospect of being away from my mother and father for most of the day.

'To pick up a wee bit of book learning,' he said.

'What's that?' I asked him.

'They'll teach you to read and write and do sums,' he explained.

'You can teach me all that, Daddy, can't you?' I pleaded with him.

'A wee bit of poetry, maybe, but . . .'

'Isn't that enough?' I butted in. I was ill at ease and the spun-out hum of a fly trapped in a jumble of books on the dresser didn't help.

'It wasn't enough for Robbie Burns, mind you,' he said cautiously and drummed a finger on the table as if trying to find a rhythm for his words. 'Poetry! You can't live on it and can't live without it.' He leaned back in his chair and gave me an attentive look. 'Poetry is dandy, but you need something more solid, a wee job you can rely on.'

'Isn't poetry a job?'

'It would be the best job in the world if you could make a living out of it,' he said.

It was a calm evening and the fresh stink of dung came to us from the midden below the house. He sniffed the air and looked out through the open doorway, his ear cocked to one side as if listening to something from afar. When I saw a twinkle in his eyes I knew that a thought had come to him.

'The funny thing is this; the poet needs to be dead before the poetry comes to life. Look at Burns. He died without a penny to his name and now two hundred years or so later his poetry is making a small fortune.' He gave me a mischievous little grin. 'You can't make a living when you're dead,' he said and chuckled loudly.

'I want to make poems, Daddy,' I blurted out excitedly, more to amuse him than anything else, but when I said it I knew that it was the truth.

He swept me off my feet and raised me high above his head. 'You'll want a bit of schooling for that, sir,' he said playfully as he held me aloft, legs dangling in the air, my face close to his.

'I suppose so,' I said, enjoying the floaty feeling of being adrift in the air.

'Well, that's settled,' he said, and swished me around in a big, flapping whirl of delight. 'You'll start in the morning.'

The teacher, a thin, bony woman in a black fleecy skirt and a dull red patterned cardigan, sat on a spindly stool in front of my class and glared at us with unblinking eyes. I sat, crouched low in my seat in clammy fear and wished my father would come to take me home. This was my first day at school, and, if I could help it at all, it would most certainly be my last.

There would be no codding about, she said, no giving cheek to the teacher and no gabbing to each other. Mischief-makers, she said, would be punished. She swished a sally rod in the air and then thwacked it impatiently against her skirt, giving little oohs and aahs of agony to show how painful it was to get a lash of it. We were to sit up straight, be on our best behaviour and always, always pay attention to what she was saying. In this room, she was the *máistreás,* the mistress, and when she spoke all eyes and ears were to be fixed on her. Earlier, when she had gone out to the porch to meet somebody, a boy in the first class told me that she was 'a sub', standing in for the real teacher who was out sick. 'She's nice,' he said and I wasn't sure which of them he meant by that.

After she rattled on a bit she had a habit of clamping her mouth shut and then baring her clenched teeth. I noticed her doing it earlier when she flew into a temper with the upper class because their handwriting was, as she put it, 'no more readable than the scratch of a cat'. Now she did it again. It was like the snap of a rat trap and it made me jumpy. I wanted to flee but was too frightened of this woman whose stern gaze swept the room and kept us penned in our desks. I looked down at my lumpy, laced-up boots and knew that I was trapped.

Coming to school that morning, sitting on the crossbar of my father's bicycle, I felt so safe, his sturdy body bundled up around me like a big, hefty overcoat shielding me from the cold. It was a morning of misty drizzle; a dense haze swirled over the glen and blurred out distances. It hung in the air, it seemed to me, like lengths of soft, pale cloth that curtained us off from the big, wide world beyond the rim of the glen. On a morning when I didn't know what lay ahead of me, it was comforting to be in this closed-in world where everything had a homely familiarity about it. Even the wispy cobwebs that hung in the bushes along the road looked like Mammy's net curtains.

Close to the school, I got pins and needles in my foot so bad that my father had to let me off the bicycle and I sat on a stone wall wriggling my toes until it eased up. An old woman wearing a white apron made from flour sacks stopped to talk. She was walking a cow out to grass. When my father told her I had pins and needles, she laid her bony hand on my bare knee and kneaded it gently.

'It's the fairies giving your foot a wee rub down so that you'll be better able for the journey that's in front of you,' she said and gave me a big toothless smile. It didn't feel like that to me. The spiky nip of it while it lasted felt more like I was walking barefoot across the stubble field on the other side of the wall. But she sounded just like my mother with her talk of fairies, and I nodded and smiled.

Weak sunlight filtered through the windows and left a stripy grey light across the desks. At home, the tick on our bed had a similar pattern of grey streaks. Thinking about that made me drowsy and

I began to nod off, but a scolding voice in my ear woke me up with a jolt.

'Rouse yourself up, you sleepy head. This is no place for napping.'

She was still perched on the stool, her fluffy skirt puffed out around her like a clucking hen. Now she was trying to wheedle something out of us, a song, a wee poem or a story. I didn't like the wheezy cluck of her voice. It was somehow threatening and didn't reach out to envelop me the way Mammy's cuddly voice held me close and soothed me.

'Surely one of you must be able to sing a wee song?'

We sat there coughing uneasily and shuffling, at a loss what to do.

'Last year's infants were much better than you lot,' she said and looked across at a row of older children who sat blankly in their seats as if all expression had been wiped clean off their faces.

When she couldn't get a boo out of any of us, she tried another tactic. She took a packet of caramels out of her pocket and tried to woo us with sweeties. She would give a caramel, she said, to any of us who sang, recited or told a story. Barefaced, I gawked at the sweets. They made my mouth water.

Suddenly I was filled with a giddy, reckless confidence. I stood up, gripped the desk and, stiff as a stick, I stammered out that I had a poem.

'*Buachaill maith*,' she said. Good boy. She smiled and seemed pleased.

'Who taught you to say this poem?' she asked me.

'Daddy. He knows heaps of poems. He knows more poems than anybody in the world,' I said boldly. Nothing could put a damper on me now. I wanted to brag about my father. 'And when he doesn't know a poem he makes one up.'

'If he's that smart, your daddy should be a teacher.'

39

I knew from the scorn in her voice that she was trying to take me down a peg but nothing could dint the pride I had in my father.

'He is. He teaches me.' And then as pure dare I added, 'He's a great teacher.'

She stretched out her scrawny neck and eyed me sourly. 'Let me be the judge of that. Now say your poem.'

My father had taught me a lot of wee rhymes in Irish and English, nonsense verse mostly. I had hardly any English, but I was good at committing to memory anything that had a lilt to it. Now I decided on a jolly poem in English and although I didn't quite know what it meant my father always laughed his head off whenever I said it at home. I wanted to show this gruff woman how good a teacher my father was but, more than anything, I wanted to make her laugh. I shut my eyes as my father instructed me and, forgetting the world around me, abandoned myself to the sound of it. My voice swelled as I got carried away on the jaunty rhythm, the bouncy swing of the words. I delivered it out loud, clear and lively.

> Down in Aberdonia
> a darkie shovelled coal.
> The darkie shoved the shovel
> up another darkie's hole.
> Says the foreman to the darkie,
> 'If you're to shovel coal,
> you're not to shove that shovel
> up that other darkie's hole.'

When I opened my eyes, there was a raw silence for a wee while and then the upper class broke into a slow splutter of giggles and titters which soon became loud hoots of laughter. A big happy howling ha-ha spread across the classroom. It was the first time that day that any of us dared to laugh. A little piece of flaky yellow plaster came unstuck above the door and trickled down to the floor. It was a nervous giggle from the room itself, I thought, as if it wanted to break out of its heavy gloom but was too afraid of the *máistreás*. I was surprised that she wasn't laughing. She sat stock still on the stool, her face drained of colour. Then all of a sudden, she slapped her hands together furiously and yelled, *'Ciúnas!'* Silence. She swung off the stool, stepped across to the table and without warning brought her fist down on it, raising a swirl of chalk dust which made her pale face even whiter. She stood gasping for breath, then whirled around and sprang at me. She seized my hand and dragged me out of the desk.

'The cheek of you. How dare you say such a disgusting thing in front of me!'

I listened in shock. What was in my wee rhyme that offended her so much? How could my father laugh at it and this woman lose her temper over it?

'Poetry!' There was venom in her voice. 'Your father should be ashamed of himself teaching you that filth.'

It was clear I had made a mistake. I stood there wishing I could wipe away this day with a duster as easily as chalk marks from a blackboard.

'You will not make a mockery of this school.' By now I was so hot I thought my blood must be boiling. I half expected a hiss of steam to come out of my ears.

'When you leave this school you will have manners on you, remember that.' After she ranted on for a bit, she clamped her mouth shut with a fierce snap and stared at me.

Then she was off again. I stood in misery, unable to move and far too frightened to tell her that my mammy would rip bits off her for treating me this badly. Outside a horse clinked its buckles and links as it clopped by on the gravelly road. I started to say in my head a little song that my mother taught me.

> *Mo chapall beag bán*
> *Ó lios na Sí,*
> *Léim ar a dhroim*
> *Is beir or an ghaoth.*

My little white steed
from the fairy ring,
jump on its back
and catch the wind.

I kept repeating it silently while she prowled around me. It eased my mind to say it over and over but then her voice hardened, became a sharp growl that bit into me and everything became garbled and mangled.

'How dare the ignorant likes of you insult the *máistreás*!' she said and she walloped my hand with a rap of her knuckles.

This was too much for me. I shrieked and threw myself on the floor. The classroom quietened down and became strangely still. All I could hear was the clip-clop of a horse and I wasn't sure whether it was outside on the road or inside my head. At that moment I wanted to be that horse. I wanted to be out on the open road, out among all that was green and simple. I wanted to be a neigh, a gallop, a mouth grazing tall grasses. I felt peculiarly distant from the woman who stood over me. There was a tingly feeling in my bones and big flashes across my eyes. Everything within me was becoming heavier, less knowable. My body was changing shape, opening itself out to let something in. I was becoming an unstoppable, trembling bulkiness. Limb by limb I was changing; a horsiness was taking me over. I was a boy becoming a horse.

A clop of hoof beats filled my head, a whinnying sound rose out of my chest. By now I was in a frenzy, neighing loudly. I shook my hindquarters and trotted. Sometimes a black dog yelped at me but I paid no heed to it. I was a sleek white horse with a flowing mane. I couldn't restrain myself any longer. I broke into a gallop, easy at first and then faster and faster. I ran and I ran in a world of green. Struggling for breath, I reared up on my hind legs and was ready to leap a wooden barrier when I blacked out and fell.

All is muzzy after that. I recall sitting by the fire on the teacher's chair with her soft, grey coat blanketing me. She is telling me that I am a good boy and mopping my sweaty face with a towel. She gives me little glances of concern when she thinks I'm not looking.

It's raining. A brown squawky hen lands outside on the window ledge and huddles up out of the wet. The *máistreás* reminds me of a hen in the rain, the way she flutters about the room looking poorly with her back all hunched up and her head bowed. I can't believe it's the same snappy woman who a while ago gave me a terrible telling-off and then slapped me. Now she's running around scared and keeping an anxious eye on me. I don't feel one bit sorry for her.

I'm all out of shape. After all, I was a horse and now I have shrunk back to being a boy. As yet, skin and hair and clothes don't fit properly. Limbs and bones are many sizes too big for me. I ache. She gives me tea in a creamy mug with a blue stripe around it just like the one I have at home. That cheered me up, but when I took a sip it tasted bitter. It wasn't at all like the sweet, sugary tea my mammy made for me. Fearful of annoying her, I drank it anyway until I drained the cup. It left a stale, fusty taste in my mouth that clung to my tongue like mould. Maybe it would take hold of my words, I thought, must them up, leave a furry coat on them. I didn't want that to happen so with my teeth I raked my mouth clean and gobbed the dirt into the fire. The *máistreás* gave me a strong look and was about to say something, but didn't. She just threw her hands in the air and groaned.

At two o'clock she took me out to the gate where my father was waiting with his bicycle to take me home. By now the rain had stopped and a soft yellow glow, much the same as you would get off an oil lamp, filled the glen. My father grinned at me and it was like light spilling out over a half-door at dusk, so warm and inviting.

'How did the scholar get on today?' he asked her.

'He was a very good boy,' she said, patting me on the head and then handing me the packet of caramels. 'He even said a lovely poem for me. Didn't you?'

She looked me in the eye and I knew it was an appeal. She was calling on me to support her.

'Didn't you?' she repeated and I could feel the rising distress in her voice. I avoided her eyes and fixed my gaze on where the wet road lay bright and shiny in the sunlight. That was the way home.

It was nearly all uphill on the way back. I was too weary to walk and I hopped on the crossbar and my father, pushing the bike, wheeled me home.

'You got the first day over you, anyway,' he said encouragingly as we left the school behind us and faced into the braes.

'I'm not going back,' I shouted and I could see the let-down look in his eyes.

'Surely it wasn't that bad?' he said softly, and pulled aside to let McFadden's grocery van go past. It swerved from side to side to avoid the potholes and soured the air with puffs of hot, thick smoke.

'The *máistreás* reared up on me,' I told him when the van had gone, groaning up the brae.

'I see. Maybe you were bold.' He broke off and grimaced at me teasingly.

'No, I wasn't but the teacher was,' I chipped in, a little vexed that he wasn't taking me seriously. 'She didn't like my poem.'

'You said a poem!' His eyes widened and he raised his head to the sky. A bright horsey cloud with a long sleek tail passed over us, heading for Errigal.

'Aye, that "Down in Aberdonia" one,' I replied. He looked at me in amazement and then his face creased up in a yelp of laughter.

'Man dear, that takes the biscuit. I bet that one gave her a right good tickle.'

I jerked my head up and glared at him. 'It wasn't funny, Daddy. She hit me.'

'She hit you, *a chroí*?' I watched him frown in disbelief. I nodded, too upset to speak.

'She's a dry shite thon one; a wee bit of devilment would slacken her up.' He tilted the bike a little, threw a leg over the saddle and we whooshed downhill.

In the dip at the bottom before we began the steep climb up Mags Brae, he turned to me. 'She couldn't be that cruel, could she?'

'She was savage, Daddy.'

'She hit you, *a chroí*, because of the poem?' and he said it in such a soft, sympathetic way that I burst out crying.

'She did, but I turned myself horsey to get away from her.' I hurried the words out in a blub of sobs.

'Holy Mother of God, she had no right to do that.'

'And then my legs gave up and I fell into black.'

There was a stunned silence. 'You passed out?' His kind, browny eyes searched my face. They were wet like speckled stones on the road.

We trudged on in silence. I could see that he was pondering what to do. 'You wouldn't wish that on a dog on his first day at school.' He gave me a wee smile and I knew it was to stop me from crying.

'I don't care a rap, Daddy. I'm not going back.'

He sighed, pushed back his cap to cool his sweaty brow and muttered as if to himself. 'By cripes, he's not going back 'til I sort this out.'

I was happy when I heard that. McFadden's van left a drizzle of petrol in the puddles on the road. Oily rainbows, they shimmered beautifully.

My mother was bent over the table when we got home, taking up the hem of a bright blue dress that Auntie Biddy had sent from Glasgow.

'I was giving it a wee nip and a tuck so that I'd be turned out like a lady for your coming home . . .'

'You're lovely, Mammy,' I butted in excitedly, and threw my arms round her waist. She wore an old green dress that had all the Mammy smells I wanted. I buried my nose in its sweet comforts and breathed it in.

'There, there,' she said, gently stroking my forehead. 'I missed you.'

'I'm not going back,' I moaned, and blurted out what

happened. She flew into a rage, snatched a knife from the table and made vicious jabs at the air.

'That bitch! I have a mind to go down and knife her,' she roared.

'Easy on, Agnes,' my father called out to her. He was sitting by the fire tamping tobacco into his pipe. 'I'll have a word with her myself.'

'A word,' she jeered. 'Damn good a word will do.' Her eyes flashed as if a thunderstorm rolled around her head. 'I'll flatten her.'

'You have to be canny when dealing with them teachers,' said my father. With the tongs he picked up a red coal from the fire, held it cautiously over the bowl and lit his pipe. 'They have all the rights on their side . . .'

'She has no right to lay a hand on my child without my say-so,' my mother cut in angrily. My father gave a resigned shrug and puffed on his pipe slowly. I got the rich smell of tobacco and snuffled with pleasure. My mother thought I was weeping.

'My wee dote,' she said and peered down at me anxiously. 'I'd kill that rip but it would only dirty the knife.' She gave a faint smile and left the knife down on the table. Then she took me in her arms and held me tightly.

'My wee dote, my wee dote.' I snuggled into the heaving warmth of her bosom. It was like resting your head on two soft, tubby puppies. I looked up at her and she smacked a kiss on my cheek. Her hair was pulled back smoothly and knotted up in a bun at the back of her head, showing off the creamy full moon of her face. A fine line of freckles stretched across her nose like a single line of sheep I sometimes saw on a clear night stepping across the moon. I was so glad that she was my mammy. My belly rumbled loudly and she heard it.

'Och, you must be starving.' She had a pot of *brúitín* – mashed potatoes – ready on the hob. She spooned it out on a plate and shaped it up into a low mound with a hole in the middle. She poured hot milk into this wee pit and topped it with a yellowy dollop of homemade butter.

I dug into it with relish, dipping each spoonful of hot mush into the buttery milk. It was delicious. When I asked for a second helping, she beamed.

'Thanks be to God but there's no bother with your stomach.' She piled my plate with another steaming heap.

'You'd eat a farmer's arse through a whinbush, wouldn't you,' she joked, 'and then have him give you his wife's leg for a meat tea on Friday.'

'I wonder what the *máistreás* would make of you, Agnes,' my father said, smiling sweetly at her.

I knew for sure the teacher would be angry with her because my mother speaks whatever comes into her head, and that wouldn't do at school. At home you could mess about with words, but at school you had to hold them back; keep them in check in case they upset the *máistreás*. I was thinking this to myself while the two of them guffawed happily by the fire. She was pouring a thick, black treacly liquid from a bottle into her cup and filling it up with hot water from the kettle.

'Does any of youse want a wee drop of coffee?' she says, slipping each of us a coy little glance, knowing that we both hate the stuff.

'It's rat's pish, Mammy,' I tell her, making a big show of throwing up. My father turns to me and I can see a slow smile curling at the corners of his mouth.

'You'll have to clean up your tongue before you go back to school.'

I giggle and put on another show of being sick.

'Do youse know what I'm going to tell youse?' my mother says, corking the black bottle and leaving it on the table beside my leftovers. 'Thon bitch in the school is as thick as *brúitín* in a bottle.'

After my father had a talk with the *máistreás* I was talked into going back to school.

He and Mammy would get into fierce trouble with the law, he stressed, if they didn't send me to school. Then the authorities would take me away and put me in a home for boys because Mammy and Daddy, they would rule, weren't fit to rear me properly.

However unwilling I was to go back to school, the thought of the law butting into our lives brought me around.

I remembered the time a policeman in a stiff cap, with bright steely buttons on his dark-blue uniform and bicycle clips in his trousers, knocked on our door. There was a weighty-looking baton belted to his tunic. I must have been about four because Granda was alive at the time and foothering about the house. When the garda arrived, he addressed Granda.

'Oo hav thistles in your field, Mr Sharkey,' he said in a thick, barbed voice that sprung at you like brambles. Granda, trying to be funny, smiled up at him.

'I tried to keep them down, sir, but the wee folk, you see, come out at night to open their bowels and whatever damn power's in their shite, them thistles grow at a wild fast rate.'

'Listen here to me,' and he crooked a long finger at Granda and scowled. 'Don't oo give me any of dat auld codology or I'll have oo up for a breach of the peace.' He loosened his belt by a notch and stood up straight in his navy blue. Built like a bullock, he was the full of the doorway. I was hoping that Granda wasn't going to quarrel with him. 'Now I'm warning oo – get rid of them noxious weeds or oo'll be fined.'

Granda nodded. 'Aye, sir, I'll cut them back to the year dot.'

'Listen, oo.' He eyed Granda up and down severely. 'Am I hearing a bit of impudence?' I noticed his ears. They were nearly as big as the handles on our enamel milk jugs. With ears like that, I suspected he heard everything. 'Are oo listening to me?'

'O, begod, aye sir,' Granda said gleefully. 'I'm hearin' you sound as a pound.'

'Make sure oo hav dat field cleaned up before I'm back this way.' He craned his neck and peeped into the kitchen, where Mammy and me stood holding hands. I could see him take stock of everything. 'Good day,' he said gruffly and off he went up the lane. I stood at the door and listened to the slithery click–click of his bike as he pedalled off into the evening.

'Och, holy shite,' my mother hissed, wagging her finger furiously at Granda. 'You'll have us all put in the lock-up, you eejit.'

That policeman frightened me. I knew that he could come back to lift me for not going to school. The horror of being shut away, far from my mother and father, was too terrible to think about, and yet I thought about it, over and over, picking at it like a scab you can't keep away from until it festers. The only cure was to go back to school.

'We have to go through what's in front of us,' my father used to say. On that basis I went back to school, but vowed never again to say a poem in class.

I was turning all of this over in my head as I sat in a heavily scratched desk at the back of the class on the day I returned to school. The *máistreás* made no fuss over me and that suited me fine. She neither snubbed me, nor did she go out of her way to notice me. I was left to meld in and become one with a bobbing mass of biddable faces. The wind drew in big sucks of breath as it scurried around the yard and gave nothing away. Against the window, a damp sky was losing colour.

We had a well below the house.

It was hidden in a ferny nook underneath a dry stone wall. You had to kneel down on a flat stone, dip the bucket into it and haul up the water. When I carried it in a white enamel pail, it became a breathy shininess that sloshed about and brimmed over like a shoal of silver fish.

On sunny days, the light gave it a coat of dazzle, making it into a shiny mirror. On those days, thirsty for a drink, I'd lie on my belly and slurp up my own face out of its cool sweetness. It was a moist cave with the same sweet-sour odour I got off my mother when I laid my head in her lap; a damp fragrance that was oddly comforting. Mossy green at the sides and rust-red where, at the back, a gurgle of water spilled out of a rock, it was a restful place to put your head into.

On no account would my mother allow water to be carried into the house after dark. It was unlucky. At night it was better to stay away from the well, she advised me. During the daytime it was ours, but at night it belonged to the '*slua sí*', the fairies. Anything could happen to you there, she stressed, at that uncanny hour.

'Look at what happened to Domhnall na Gealaí,' she warned me. Domhnall was a youngster who always went to the well at night to fetch a bucket of water, against his mother's better judgement it must be said. One night, the moon whooshed down, seized him and carried him off to the sky. On clear nights, I could make him out, standing at a crossroads, a sack on his back, staring blankly ahead. I felt sorry for him, all alone on that lonely moon. Sometimes I'd point a torch at him and flash a friendly wave just to show him that somebody was thinking about him. I wondered could my wee light really slash at the dark and make a bright path up through the night to where he stood, dithering over which road to take. But now and again a flicker in his glassy eye was enough to convince me that contact was being made. As well as that, having a nodding acquaintance with Domhnall na Gealaí made that far-off moon seem less distant.

From time to time my father and I cleaned out the well. With tin buckets, we drained it dry and then scooped up the ooze and slobber that clotted the bottom of it. 'Clear water comes from a clean well,' he'd tell me. 'Aye, boy, you've to care for the source.' He always threw in a sprinkling of lime to purify it. 'Always think of the well when you're drinking the water,' he would counsel me.

Once, when we were bucketing out the well, he tossed the water in a wide arc behind him and created one glittering rainbow after another.

'How do you make a rainbow, Daddy?' I asked him, astounded at what was happening in front of me.

'I don't rightly know,' he said modestly. He peered around as if groping for an answer. Across the glen, a pale sun shivered behind damp clouds. 'I just fling the water at the sun,' he said and laughed at the simplicity of it. I wanted to be a rainbow-maker too, just like my daddy. I took my bucket in my hands and flung the water up into the air the way he was doing it but no matter how much I tried, it wouldn't rainbow for me. Again with an easy swerve, he slung the water out and up and instantly it curved into a glowing bow of colours. Frustrated, I broke out sobbing.

'Why can't I do it, Daddy?' I complained bitterly.

'Och, I don't know, *a thaisce*,' and he gave me a mournful look.

'It's just pot luck,' he said, trying to console me. 'You throw it in the air and if you're lucky, it catches the light. It's all in the slant, I think, and the timing.'

He suggested we try it together. We gripped the bucket, my father on one side, me on the other. 'Righto,' he urged and we tossed the glistening water into the air, and for one magical moment it flared up into a flashy rainbow and then was gone. Brief but perfect. We looked at each other in wonder.

'We made a rainbow, Daddy!'

'Aye, boy, a well-made rainbow, you could say,' and he guffawed delightedly at his own wordplay. Brimming with joy, I also broke out laughing. Something strange had happened, I felt, at that moment, something delicately rare and pure as if we had overflowed into one another.

We tried it again but never managed to make a second rainbow. Soon, the evening light waned and gave way to dusk and then, like net curtains being drawn, a fine drizzle closed around us.

I loved the sound of the Angelus as it chimed its way down the glen from the church in Dunlewey. Sometimes, if the evening was still, and my mother wasn't looking, I would scramble up a big ash tree that grew on the rise behind our henhouse and wait in the hush for that rounded sound to sweep down the glen. I had to be careful. If my mother caught me out I would get into fierce trouble. The first time I climbed the tree I lost my nerve halfway up and didn't dare budge. I gripped a branch and yelled my head off to get attention. When, at last, she managed, somehow, to huckster me down on her shoulders, she gave me a terrible clout across the face.

'You ramscooter, you haven't a splink of sense to be going up a tree like that. If ever I catch you at that caper again, I'll give you a welt you won't be the better of for a week.' My mother, when she was really angry, yelped like a mad dog.

Up in the tree, I felt closer to the lovely chimes that rippled the air. It was bliss. I was floating on a roll of sound. The Players fags that my father smoked had a picture of a bearded sailor in a peaked cap framed inside a lifebelt. The round sound of the Angelus reminded me of that lifebelt. The buoyancy of it gave me a lift, cheered me up. I floated off on it across the fields and the bogs and out and up to the blue beyond of the evening hills.

One very clear and still evening, I ventured higher than usual. A cackling magpie perched on the henhouse roof cleared its throat. Below me, I could see a willy wagtail skip along a wall that was covered in crawling briars. Betty, our cow, grazed a green patch at the foot of the tree. My father was out in the yard with an upturned bicycle, patching a rip on the tyre. Earlier, my mother took a dander up the road to visit a neighbour. Across the glen I could see where the tinkers had camped in a sheltered hollow by the wayside. Their hooped tent was made of brown sacking and beside it, a bright-red horse-drawn caravan. A white horse tethered to a paling post neighed loudly.

Earlier that day, I wandered off down the fields and kept going till I reached the river. I didn't expect anyone to be there and I was taken aback by a tinker boy sitting on the bank, his trousers rolled up and his feet dangling in the water. I was frightened and wanted to run for it but he saw me before I could make off. I stood there, rooted to the ground. Making a break for it was no good, I knew, he would easily catch me with his long, striding legs. I was seven and he was, maybe, double that age.

He smiled and patted the ground at his side, signalling that I should sit beside him. Alone with a stranger, and a tinker at that, I didn't know what to do. I was shaking with fear. Everybody was wary of the tinkers, and would have nothing to do with them except buy their tin wares, now and again: their cans, their pandies, and their buckets. They had a bad name for thieving and pulling a fast one over on you.

'Them feckin' tinkers would swindle you out of your own shadow if you weren't lookin',' I heard Nora John say the day before when they tried to get her to sell a lovely cuckoo clock she had for half nothing.

They had rough accents, shifty eyes and bad smells and they frightened me whenever they came to our house. They eyed things up and down as if planning to come back and rob us.

He was still smiling and beckoning me to come to him. Haltingly, one step at a time, I moved towards him. He reached out for my hand and gently pulled me down beside him on the grassy bank. He tousled my hair, put his arm around my shoulder and gave me a big grin, full of black, chipped teeth. I couldn't make head or tail of anything he said. I knew it was English but it sounded like a dog slurping water. After a little while he unlaced my boots, took them off, and then my stockings. I was afraid he was going to keep them but I didn't have the guts to stop him. Instead, he stood up in the shallow water and began to splash it on my feet and wash them. The cool tingle of it was pleasant on my skin and when he rubbed it in between my toes he tickled me and made me giggle. When he bent down with his back to me to bathe them properly, I saw his thin, patchy trousers tighten across his sturdy bum and that excited me. I had a strong desire to touch him there and then, but before I could do anything about it, he straightened up and began to dry my feet with a strip of faded red cloth which he used as a hanky. He helped me pull on my socks and then he tied my shoes. He doubled up the laces neatly around the upper part of the boots and knotted them into a fancy bow.

We sat in silence for a while watching the flow. I had to get back home because it was time for dinner. I pointed up to the house to let him know that I had to go and he nodded his head to show me he understood. It was when he began to walk that I noticed how unsteady he was on his feet. He dragged one leg behind him like a cripple. Now I was glad I didn't run away from him. At the top of the field I turned around to give him a wave but he was already hobbling off through the bog up to his tent.

Up in the tree, I'm trying to make him out from the blur of faces sitting around a smoky fire in front of their encampment. To see better, I risk a branch on the brink. As the Angelus bell rang out, it swayed beneath me and then snapped. I crashed through the springy branches and landed with an almighty whack on the back of Betty, still grazing at the bottom. Lucky for me she broke my fall. For an instant, she slumped, then leapt wildly in the air, snorting and frothing. I clutched her ears and held on firmly while she bounded across the yard and headed through the wooden gate leading down to her byre. When she rammed the gate, I shot through the air and soft-landed on a mound of dry dung which my father had shovelled out of an old sheep shed that he was repairing. Now, I saw him come running towards me, his face white as a sheet. Stunned, he stood looking at me, half buried in the muck. When I smiled up at him, he gave a long sigh of relief and blessed himself.

'God, you gave me the fright of my life,' he said, still shaken by what he had witnessed. I was unharmed except for a few scratches on my face and legs and a coating of stinking grime on my clothes. Riding the cow like a rodeo-man and being flung off her back was strangely exhilarating. It was a dangerous thrill and I wanted to experience it again and again; that mad frothing dash and then the headlong hurl through the air into the unknown.

Father took me into the kitchen, washed me down, daubed Dettol onto my bleeding wounds and then got me to change my clothes. He was more upset by what had happened than I was and in a trembling voice kept telling me how lucky I was to be alive.

The next morning while still in bed, I heard a loud creaking groan outside and then something crashing heavily to the ground. I jumped out of bed, threw on some clothes in a hurry, and rushed out to see what happened. My father stood with a saw in his hand and looked grimly at the toppled tree. It must have cut him to the quick to do what he did because he himself hated to see anybody mistreat a tree. We looked at each other and neither of us uttered a word. I was the cause of that tree being cut down and I felt bad about it.

I knelt down and told it I was sorry. It had gone all limp and no longer stirred in the breeze. I looked across the glen but there were no tinkers. They had already packed up and left. I wanted to meet that boy again and be alone with him by the river. It didn't matter that he was a tinker, I liked him but now he was gone.

I walked away and into a tangle of trees by the cow byre. I sat down in the shade; a damp, watery light shone on my shoes and in the hush I could hear my heart toll like a bell.

My mother had no interest whatsoever in books but my father was always absorbed in one. She would scold him if he was reading, especially in the middle of the day.

'You have little to do stuck in them books and that braddy cow of Andy's ready to leap into our turnips.'

My father would raise his head from the book and give her an oddly vacant look.

'Will you chase her away yourself, *a stór*. I'm in the middle of the Battle of the Somme.'

'Och, yerself and them bloody books,' she'd say and shake her head disdainfully. Then she would dash out the door and do whatever had to be done.

In a townland where nobody had books, our house was the exception. My father's interests were, for the most part, history and poetry and the sizeable stack of books piled high on our dresser were mainly histories of the First World War, the collected works of Robbie Burns, William Wordsworth, Robert Service and the novels of Patrick McGill. My father, although he never progressed beyond the fifth class at primary school was, by virtue of his bookish tendencies, considered to be quite a scholar by some of the locals. There were others who regarded the reading of books as a complete waste of time and judged my father to be an idler.

One Sunday evening, dodging at our gable, listening to some local men who were having a yarn at the bend in the road above our house, I heard one of them, a man who was known for making cutting remarks about his neighbours, say, in a sneery voice, 'Sharkey is a heedless man. He's down there gawking at books and his farm coming to nothing. You can plough a field, y'see, but you can't plough a book.' The others laughed at that. I was raging and wanted to give him his comeuppance. I stood out and barked up at him, 'My daddy can read a book and that's one thing you can't do, stupid.'

There was a sudden lull in the talk and, one by one, the men sneaked away awkwardly. 'That youngster is as mad as the streel of a mother he has,' I heard him say contemptuously as they took themselves off up the road out of earshot.

When I told my father what had happened, he just smiled and said, 'The poor man has a grudge against life. When he says things like that he's just grumbling about his own life.' My father wasn't a man to lash out at anybody or take them to task. 'Never judge anyone 'til you have walked a mile in their shoes,' he used to say as a gentle rebuke to my mother whenever she bad-mouthed a bothersome neighbour or gave out about a relative.

Nights when rain skittered down the windows and rough gusts howled around the house, I'd roll up in his lap and listen to the whine and suck of the wind rattling in our chimney. It was a winged horse, he'd tell me, from a land far away, coming with a poem for me. What we were hearing was the clank of its buckles and links. And then he'd ask me to cock an ear and listen closely. Maybe we could make out the poem it was saying. Of course in that stirred-up state I heard words, 'wind-words' we called them and together we'd piece them into a poem. A poem that was a sheer delight of sound without any recourse to meaning:

Yom strom karum num no
Tun du aru glob glob o

When I was doing this, I felt that my tongue was in flame like the lit-up wick in our globed oil lamp. At the time we didn't have electric light in the house. It was either a tilly or a paraffin lamp. The tilly was a contrary light, its frail, lacy mantle liable to disintegrate at the slightest touch. It hissed like a gander and looked like one too with its plump body and scraggly neck. The oil lamp, although its glow was dimmer than the tilly, was more convenient to light. I could even do it.

Sometimes my father would take me with him when he went for a ramble at night to a neighbouring house. Occasionally we visited Niall and Neddie, two kindly, bachelor brothers who lived about a twenty-minute walk from our house. Laurel and Hardy, he called them fondly. Niall was big-boned and thick-set while Neddie was small and sprightly. While Neddie talked, Niall pottered about the house, humming some out-of-tune song to himself. Something in Neddie's delivery as he told us stories, his chuckling speech like a rushing stream, made my ears tingle.

Niall's speech came in puffs and pants like the plumping kettle on the fire. On the first night that he brought me to their house, Neddie told me that the world would end in fire. 'It'll all go up in flames,' he said with great certainty. 'The sky above us will be red hot and the stars drippin' like bits of burning rubber.' He paused and pulled at his pipe thoughtfully.

That horrified me out of my wits. When I went out for a pee – and I was very reluctant to go but was too ashamed to piddle in my pants and leave a big, wet dribble on their dry floor – I only went as far as the doorstep. The sky glowed as if it were on fire. I pissed quickly and was buttoning up my trousers when it happened. A big chunk of burning something flashed across the sky and fizzled out above Dunlewey. And then another one, bigger and brighter, hurled through the night. I rushed in screaming that the world was coming to an end.

Startled, they jumped off their seats and ran to the door to see what in the heavens above had panicked me so much. The sky was chilly bright with twinkling stars but there wasn't a flame in sight. When I told them what I'd seen, they burst out laughing.

'You saw two falling stars, *a thaisce*,' Neddie explained to me. 'Two souls on their way to heaven.'

For weeks after that I dreamt that the sky was falling down in fiery drips. I'd wake up shaking with fear and my father had to carry me to the window to convince me that the sky was still up there and that the moon and the stars were all solidly in place.

My father is on the floor on all fours, and I'm astride him, riding high and happy. He trots hoppity-hop along the flagstones, doing the round of the kitchen. He neighs and then lets on to be champing the bit and rattling his harness. I hold on tightly to the reins of his galluses, click my tongue and tease him forward. 'Giddy up, Betty. Giddy up, horsey.' He speeds up into a gentle gallop, then all of a sudden stalls and I come tumbling off his back in skraiks of laughter.

'You call yourself a cowboy, do ye?' he taunts me, then sits me on his knees and tickles me absently, half-heartedly, as if his attention is elsewhere. Usually, I'm pleading for mercy, his tickling is so lively and vigorous. When I look at him I notice that something is amiss in his face; it has lost its colour, its ruddy glow. It has become pale grey and pasty like the dough Mammy makes.

'I'm going away to Scotland tomorrow,' he says cautiously.

Scotland, although I didn't know where it was exactly, was a place that was familiar to me. I had heard so much about it from my parents, who had worked there before they were married. I knew that it was a place where people went, men mostly, when they needed work. Nevertheless, it took me by surprise. The disclosure was so sudden, so strange and dangerous. I was dropped in the middle of no place and in the dark of night left to wander where there was no light and no human warmth.

'When will you be back?' I asked, rubbing the rough, spiky stubble on his jaw with a nervous finger.

'In five months or thereabouts,' he said.

'How long is five months, Daddy?' He gave a soft sigh and his eyes moistened.

'Not too long, *a chroí*, when you're out playing every day.'

My heart was in a flutter as if a little bird was trapped in my ribcage. I could hear the dip and rise of it and I thought it was going to burst out through my mouth any minute. That night, lying between them in bed, I held on to my father with a pressing neediness, not wanting to lose the warm sureness of his presence. I wished that the night would dawdle, linger here and there, mooch about in the moonlight and forget about the morning. I was annoyed at the tick-tock urgency of the clock ushering in the dawn. When the light began to seep through a chink in the curtains, a feeling of hopelessness came over me. Daylight would take him away from me.

There was a cold nip in the air when I went out to pee behind the house. The sun was like a shiny copper penny standing on its edge above Andy's Hill. I knew that my father was going to Scotland to earn some money so that we wouldn't be as hard up as we were. Nearly all the neighbouring men went; that was how things were for grown-ups, I guessed. Taking the Derry boat was part of their lives. I wished that we weren't so poor; then my father wouldn't have to go away. I prayed that, somehow, we would fall into money; that a legacy would, unexpectedly, come our way. Didn't my Auntie Mary in Mín Doire na Slua say that we had rich relatives in faraway Montana? I asked God would He mind taking one of them up to heaven, but not before they had left us a big lab in their will. The fierce squawk of a crow as it swished out of the trees behind the henhouse frightened me, and I scampered back to the kitchen. Maybe it was a sign of disapproval from God for demanding such an awful thing, but then again it could have been a hint that He had given the go-ahead to my desperate request.

My mother was up and doing her best to be cheerful, but sometimes her words faltered and she'd turn away and wipe her eyes with the hem of her apron. She made porridge and sweetened mine with a more-than-usual sprinkling of sugar. I began to like the rasp and scratch of her spoon as she scraped the pot for '*scriobogaí*', the burnt scourings that my father liked. Every other morning the grind of it grated on my nerves, but now it was a sound I associated with him and it was comforting. His early-morning clatter around the house usually woke me up and left me grumpy. Now I was going to miss all that morning din of his, the creek of byre doors opening and closing and the racket of tin buckets in the yard as he tended the cattle.

We sat around the fire eating Mammy's stodgy porridge and chatting about the journey that he was about to make. Talking settled my nerves and distracted me. He would take the Loch Swilly bus to Derry, he said, have a bite and a sup in Molloy's, close to the Diamond, and then sail on the *Lairds Lough*, a cattle ship to Glasgow. He would stay for a day or two with Auntie Biddy in Ballater Street and then head on up to Haddington by bus. He knew all the farms around there and would easily find work. I longed to see the little towns whose names tripped off my father's tongue like fabulous enchantments: East Linton, Stenton, Chirnside, Dunbar, Duns, Grantshouse. And the farms themselves – Beanston Mains, Harelaw, Morkel, Belgrange, The Knowes, Abbey Mains – were magical domains, ablaze with the rich yield of their wheat fields. When he talked about handling horses I could hear the trot and clatter of Clydesdales across cobbled farmyards. He told me that a single potato field in Beanston Mains was as big as all the fields of Mín A Leá rolled into one.

After breakfast, my mother stood on a chair and took down the dingy, brown cardboard suitcase that was stored atop the high press in the bedroom, dusted it off and began to pack it with 'Daddy's ould duds', as she said: his brown corduroy trousers, a bulky gansey, some shirts and an old tweed jacket, his *bainín* waistcoat and a pair of scruffy, hobnailed boots which she scrubbed clean before putting them in. At ten o'clock, clean-shaven and wearing his Sunday best – a light-blue, double-breasted suit, a crisp white shirt and a cap – he was ready to leave.

When we faced each other to say farewell, I thought the floor was quaking under me. Everything was in a hopeless wobble. He clasped my hand and said, 'You're the man of the house now. Be good to Mammy and look after her, won't you?'

'Cheerio, Daddy. I'll be thinking of you every day,' I gulped out, at a loss for words.

'I'll write as soon as I get settled on a farm, Agnes,' he said, hugging my mother who was now weeping loudly.

He lifted the battered suitcase and walked out, head down and expressionless, without looking at us. We stood in the doorway watching him go. At the cow byre, he turned around and waved. The sun shone on his scrubbed face and we could make out big smudges on his cheeks. He was crying. Then he hopped over a ditch and was gone.

An old pair of his tweed trousers hung limp on a hook behind the kitchen door. I buried my head in them and cried my eyes out. Afterwards, I felt that a little bit of me fell away and disappeared in the tears the way a small peaty *bruach* collapsed sometimes and fell into the Dúloch, the Black Lake. That was what people meant by loss. You lost something of yourself and you had to replace it with something else; otherwise you drained away and shrivelled up.

One Saturday, soon after my father went away, a stranger came to our house. I remember a wispy twilight mist coiling itself around us as we greeted him in our yard. Like a wraith, it moved in chilly spirals and made me shiver.

'I'm looking for a pump, missus,' he said in a rash, giddy voice, his leery eyes raking my mother up and down. He was scruffy and had a tangle of black, snarly hair. When he belched, I could smell the stink of drink off his heavy breath.

'There's no pump here. You'll have to try our neighbours over there, they have a bicycle,' my mother said curtly. With that, she dismissed him. We hurried into the house and bolted the door. We watched him from behind the kitchen curtains as he loitered there, taking stock of everything.

'I don't like the look of that fella at all,' she said, as he shuffled off up the lane. She sensed danger and I knew it. I was out in a cold sweat but tried hard to keep my fear at bay for her sake.

That night, around ten o'clock as we were preparing for bed, we heard a rattle at our door. It was a low persistent rap at first, then a loud knock and a thump. I got the jitters and screamed.

'What do you want?' my mother called out boldly.

'A good pumping, missus.'

It was him alright and he spoke in a slurred, groggy voice. We were in for it, I thought, and nobody to defend us.

'Go away out of that, you dirty git.'

My mother was determined to stand her ground and brazen him out with her gutsy defiance. She stood, her hands on her hips, and all of a sudden grew in stature. We could hear him walking away from the door, then the sudden rush and heave as he slammed into it with full brute force. Lucky for us, it was a sturdy wooden door fastened securely to a solid frame. My father had made it the year before.

'It's made to last,' he had said proudly. 'The house'll fall before the door does.'

I was so scared, I stood there stony still.

'Don't stand there like a paling post. Here, give me a hand and we'll huckster this to the door.' She got hold of one end of our hefty table, me at the other end, and between us we dragged it down the floor and bolstered it up against the door. We piled two sackfuls of dry turf which we kept in the house for the kitchen and bedroom fires on top of that as extra reinforcement. She also took out the graip and the pitchfork which were kept in the pantry for safekeeping alongside the spade and the shovel, and Daddy's set of carpentry tools.

'Open up, will ye?' he growled from outside.

'I'll open you up with the graip if you dare come near me, you scut,' my mother roared at him. I wasn't sure whether she was genuinely unafraid or just putting on a bold front to prop me up, but I was encouraged by how she was standing up to this fearful ordeal. My mammy had real pluck.

Our house had only one door and two small sash windows. In his drunken state, I reasoned, it was unlikely that he'd attempt to enter by the window. If he did, we had the graip and the pitchfork at the ready to bloody him up a bit if that was necessary.

He rammed into the door a few times. The jolt and creak when he hit it made me shudder, but I was not going to give in. It was the edgy pauses, the tense waiting between batterings, that keyed me up and knotted my stomach. On his last charge, he stumbled on loose gravel and banged his head against the doorway. He gave a great yelp of pain and slumped heavily against the door. We prayed that he was knocked out. Next, we heard loud croaky snores as if a pool full of frogs inhabited our doorway.

'He's scuttered, thank God,' my mother said. Then she came up with a daring plan. She persuaded me to sneak out the bedroom window, make a dash to our neighbours and alert them to what was happening. As I jumped from the window onto the grass verge of the path, I was all ears and toes. In the moonlight, I saw the dark hulk heaped on our doorstep. He was sound asleep. Usually, I dreaded the dark. Any little movement would have startled me, but this night I kept my composure and didn't scare. I was on a mission to save my mother and nothing was going to daunt me. I rapped up the neighbours and got three men with sticks and lanterns to come to our house.

They recognised the intruder, a man from further down the glen, they said, who had a reputation for harassing women. When my mother heard the commotion outside, she yanked the table out of the way and stood in the doorway holding a tin basin.

'A good scoosh of cold water will put him in his right mind,' and she sloshed the water over his head. With a sudden jerk, he sat upright and found himself surrounded by three dangling hurricane lamps. He looked lost and dazed in the yellowed light. The men hauled him to his feet and poked the sticks threateningly in his face. He had sobered up, and looked like a frightened animal caught in the glare of light.

'Scaring women and children in the night is no carry-on. If you don't be off now, you latchico, we'll give you a scutching you'll never forget,' one of the men said, shoving him up the lane. We followed him at a distance to make sure that he was on his way.

Later that week, we heard that a woman further down the glen whose husband was away in Scotland was also being pestered by him. A few nights before when he came battering at her door, she was prepared. She opened it and flung a bucket of scalding hot water at him, burning him to the bone. The neighbours heard his howls of pain as he made off down the road.

After that red-hot scorching, he never bothered us again but, sometimes, I'd wake up from a bad dream in which he was entering our house with an evil leer on his face.

Shortly after that, Uncle Joe, my mother's brother from Mín Doire na Slua, a stout, simple-minded man who plodded along at his own slow pace and smiled at the sky, came to keep us company. It was safer to have a man in the house, my mother said, although Joe was more of a spoilt child than a man. His big, droopy face had the grey pallor of candle grease and indeed looked as if it were going to drip down at any minute, feature by feature. His nose, which he kept scratching, was ragged with blackheads and red and the only bit of colour in an otherwise waxy complexion. His slit, muddy-coloured eyes reminded me of wee bird-ruts in wet gravel.

My mother had to keep him in cigarettes. Without them he became cranky and howled like a chained dog. There was always a fag dangling from the corner of his mouth. He never puffed on it, he just let it burn down to a butt and then he flicked a match and lit up another one. A spattering of ashes always flecked up the front of his dark clothes.

He was mostly useless about the house and couldn't in any way fend for himself. He couldn't light a fire, make a cup of tea, read the time, milk the cow, play cards, count money, handle a spade, shave himself or make decisions. He was strong though and could carry things: a reel of turf or fodder to feed the cattle. He could run simple errands from house to house if given clear instructions, 'Ask Nora John can she spare a wee grain of sugar 'til the grocery van comes,' or he could go to the shop if he had a list with him to give to the shopkeeper.

He didn't like Mín A Leá and never tired of telling my mother how lonely and out of the way it was.

'Agnes, this is the last place God made and he didn't have time to finish it.'

'It's not that bad, Joe,' she would plead.

'I have been around a lot of lonely corners, Agnes, but this place would make the hair stand on your head.'

When he wasn't doing the wee jobs that he could do, he just loafed about, smoked and smiled benignly at the sky.

'My father is up there. I see him every day,' he told me. Charlie Roarty, my mother's father, was murdered in Glasgow when Joe was a boy and Mary, my grandmother, had to rear a household of kids on her own without the support of a husband.

'What's he doing?' I asked him, just as a tease.

'He's doing nothing. You don't have to do anything when you are dead,' he countered and I saw a damp light flickering across his eyes.

He couldn't hold a normal conversation. In the middle of a chat, he would lapse into a vacant, forgetful silence and just stare. But sometimes he sparkled and turned out a succinct turn of phrase; a rare and apt enjambment of ideas that delighted me.

'It has room for four priests, that's how big the house is, Agnes' was how he described a larger than usual house that was being built close to where he lived.

'You couldn't make anything of that one, Agnes. She's like a bad cat in a tight bag,' was his summing-up of a rather snappish relative.

One day when we ran out of cigarettes and he was craving for a smoke, he told me as sourly as he could, 'When I don't have a fag, Charlie, I'm like a clocken hen that has no eggs under her.'

On rainy days, he wouldn't put a foot outside but would stand instead in the doorway and keep repeating, loud enough to be irritating, 'Plink-plonk! Plip-plap! Plink-plonk! Plip-plap!' He had this morbid fear that the rain would get into his ears and fill his head up with water and then he'd die from the damp.

'Will ye stop that bliddy plinkin'!' my mother would scream at him when she couldn't bear it any longer.

'Plink-plonk! Plip-plap!' He took no notice of her. He was like the rain itself. There was nothing to do but put up with it until it stopped. If the rain lasted, he'd keep up this loony refrain for hours. It got so bad one day when there was no sign of the rain ceasing, my mother wound a scarf around his mouth to gag him and stood over him with a stick to make sure he didn't utter a word or dare undo his muzzle. He was afraid of her when she was angry and did whatever she told him to do.

'When Agnes is lifted,' he used to say, 'the cups shake on the table.'

Plink-plonk! Plip-plap! I enjoyed the daftness of it up to a point but then the sheer dreary repetitiveness of it annoyed and bored me and I'd try and wrest him away from the door, either drag him out or tug him in but he was too solid to move. I had to leave him until it dried up. He'd come in then, pull a chair up to the fire and say, 'That was a damp kinda day.'

Often when the rain came, our door got swollen up with the damp so badly that it wouldn't open or shut properly without a strong pull or a good shove. Uncle Joe was like that, a swollen door in our world.

It was a clammy morning at the tail end of July. A low, grey cloud with a stippling of brown and pink hung over the hills like a distended udder. My mother was in the cow byre milking. I could hear the hum and purr of her voice as she sang a *suantraí*, a Gaelic lullaby, to settle the cows. When I was a baby she always sang that song to hush and soothe me when I cried. Now it lulled me again into a deep sense of contentment as I entered the byre and sat down beside her on a small three-legged stool. I didn't mind the cobwebbed murk of the place or the whiff of dank straw and the stench of skittery dung that filled my nostrils. It was exciting to sit close to my mother in that breathy half-light and watch her tug and squeeze those teats of mottled pink and see spurts of warm milk thwacking into the tin bucket that was wedged between her bare, bony knees. The sweaty mystery of it roused me. The jerk of teat and spew of milk done with a steady drag of the hand, the heave and slump of the cows breathing, the rise and fall of my mother's song made my heart thump in a way that I had never experienced before. I felt a hot urgency in my chest as if a bud of fire had opened up within me, a sweet, burning pressure that made me blush. Why, I didn't know. Suddenly a beat, a rhythm, a word stirred in me, a palpitating thrust as pressing as the push of a root through stodgy soil. And then the tingle and pulse of words as they gushed out of me. Cowmothermorning. Milksongbyre. Dunglightpoem. I was giving voice to something inasmuch as the gibberish I uttered meant anything. Cadence became deliverance and I felt a jolt of wild joy shooting up my body as I chanted the words out loud so that my mother, the two cows and the stones of the byre could hear them. Cowmothermorning. Milksongbyre. Dunglightpoem. The gasp and grunt of them coming out of my mouth made me tremble. I was scattering seeds in a new field, tiny grains of sound, seedlings of sense. The cows gazed at me with big, still eyes streaked with silver. My mother turned around, ripples of soft light like a hand smoothing down her thick, wavy hair. She dipped her finger in the bucket and blessed herself with the bright creamy froth. She always did that when she had finished the milking.

'Are you praying?' she said, giving me a wry smile. It hadn't occurred to me that what I was saying was a prayer. I thought of it more as a poem, but now it crossed my mind that maybe a poem and a prayer were one and the same. They were both ways of talking to God. At church they were very strict about the saying of prayers. Prayers were to be revered. They were set words, solid as holy rocks in the huge mind of God and they could not be changed. We had to say them as they were, faithfully and accurately.

'Was that a prayer, Mammy?' I asked her, startled at the idea that my own words could be one. I thought that only saints could make up prayers, pure devouts who glimpsed the sacred texts hanging in the chapels of heaven.

'I don't know, *a chroí*, but you were reelin' it off like a litany at a wake,' she said, untethering the cows and letting them out to graze around the byre. Through the open doorway a faint yellowy light glided into the byre, hovered over us and then was gone. For a moment the place glowed as if an angel had looked in on us.

When my father was working away in Scotland, he would write home and send a few quid to run the house and keep us in food. Those letters were eagerly awaited because they were the only contact we had with him while he was away in Scotland. When a letter came I always put it to my nose and breathed in its odour, hoping to get a sniff of him, a hint of his breath, a whiff of what he was wearing, a scent of tobacco smoke. And even if it was only a dry, papery smell that was enough to suggest a trace of him, maybe his grey gansey drying out by the fire in the bothy where he lived.

Although I couldn't read at this time I studied his thin wispy scrawl with great care, knowing that it was like a thread spooled out of his hand and stretching across from Scotland, bringing the three of us closer together. That made the awful gap of separation a little bit more bearable.

I was familiar enough with the ABC to recognise most of the letters, but as yet couldn't make sense of them when they were bunched up and made into words. I'd search his handwriting letter by letter and try to gauge what his feelings were as he penned them. If he was happy I noticed that he wrote in a loopy scribble, beautiful as baby curls. On the other hand if he was upset about something his writing became more of a splatter, a slosh of ink like a wave hitting off a rock.

My mother couldn't read or write so we brought the letter to Mrs G, a kind obliging neighbour, to have it read for us. We sat in silence in her cosy kitchen as she read it to the tick of two clocks and the smell of baking bread. We relished each word as if it were one of the tasty raisin scones she gave us for tea. Only one of his letters is still extant. Sent in August 1959 from Beanston Mains, it's typical of the kind of letter he wrote home.

Dear Agnes and Charlie,

I hope this letter finds you both well. I'm fine myself and out in the fields all day. We're all behind like the cow's tail with the harvest for the weather was worse than bad but now it's picked up and we're at it as long as the day is bright. It's the sort of work that tires you out but devil the bit of me cares when I'm getting paid for what I'm doing. They had me gapping hedges the days that were wet, myself and a cotter, a fly-boy who never stops bragging about himself. Some people do be mad to talk about themselves because nobody else is going to be doing it. The farmer himself is very hippity-tippidy man and likes things to be done right and no futtering about. He's always giving out to this cotter because he's slack. I'd be as happy as the day is long to be working on my own and not bothering with him at all. If he could gap up and fence the way he talks we'd have half of Scotland behind wire and blocked off by now. This last week it's fierce sunny and I'm turning the colour of yella meal from being out morning to night.

Last Saturday night the farmer and his wife who were going visiting took me in their car to Haddington. I was feeling the drought for a few beers after the long slog in the sun, and it did me good to get out of the bothy for a wee while. I met a man from over Derryconnor way and we had a bottle together. When I came here the first time with my father, God be good to him, Haddington on a Saturday night used to be mobbed with Gortahork men. There was more of them here than at home. Now there's hardly a soul about. It's so lonely it would bring tears to your eyes. Them times are gone. They're all on the buildings in England where I hear there's bings of money to be had labouring. Farm work is changing. It's nearly all done by machinery and there's no need for hired help like me who can't drive anything. Maybe next season I'll try my luck in Glasgow. I could stay with Biddy, I suppose, and get a labouring job with a contractor. Things are changing in this country. They're getting over the war and pumping money into building up the place. The war shook them up but it got money out of the banks and there's going to be good times coming.

Tell Charlie *beag* I miss him every day but he's not to be crying for me for I'll be home in no time at all and reading him all the Robbie Burns poems he likes. I know he doesn't like school and you don't mind keeping him at home, Agnes, but it's for his own betterment to go. If he doesn't have a wee grasp of education, what will become of him when he grows up? I want our wee boy to have a chance in life and without a bit of schooling there's going to be no opening for him. If he goes to school every day he'll be able to write me a letter and that'll make Daddy so happy.

You should get a lorryload of turf home and stack it in the byre and not be up and down with the creel. It's too much for your back, Agnes, all that heavy carrying. If you hurt yourself and you're laid up, who's going to care for Charlie? I have to be finishing up now, I have a few spuds and carrots on the boil and they're ready. I have a wee piece of bacon to go with them. I have to lock all the food up in my suitcase as the bothy is creeping with mice. They make some almighty racket at night but I'm too tired to care. Tell everybody at home I'm asking for them.

Send me all the news, Agnes. I'm always happy when I get your letter and know that yourself and Charlie *beag* are well. God bless all of us.

Micky

I enclose two pounds. I'm putting a wee bit aside every week to help us get through when I go home.

Once when Mrs G was not available to read the letter, my mother approached another neighbour; a pushy, waxy-faced woman in horn-rimmed glasses. It was the day McFadden's grocery van came to Mín A Leá. These travelling shops were the convenience stores of the day, door-to-door mini-marts. They were stuffed emporiums of grocery that brought all they needed, and what's more, a little novelty beside, to people living in out-of-the-way places. 'Getting the goods' was the expression in use and, in a manner of speaking, it was apt because, in addition to the necessities – tea, sugar, flour, white bread, salt – a person usually bought a wee treat if they could spare the price: a packet of biscuits, a Madeira cake, a tin of fruit, a poke of hard chewy sweets, some indulgence or other that livened up the everyday sameness of plain country fare.

The neighbours were clustered around the van waiting their turn to buy the week's provisions. My mother, clutching the letter in her hand, asked Nancy if she would oblige her by reading it whenever the van had gone. She gave a snort of disapproval and said, 'I don't have time to be reading it later. I'll do it now.' With that she snatched the letter out of my mother's hand and proceeded to read it in a loud quivery voice as if from a stage. The neighbours thought that her actressy show-off was a hoot and they laughed. My mother stood there, head bowed and sheepish. Although she had a sharp tongue, she was always hesitant and timid, diffident even, in the presence of women who could read and write. Now her nerve failed her and she remained silent.

I was furious at the nasty way this woman had put her down. Her showy insolence angered me, but I was too small to speak out and scold her.

'You'd think Micky was writing to somebody with an education,' she said, handing the letter back to my mother. I couldn't but notice the sneer on her face as she said it. However young I was, I knew that this was a slur on my mother and it hurt me. It was mean and cruel and out of order. I saw Nora John, a neighbour, cringe with shame at her offensive remark. She stared blankly at the ground and avoided my eye. Mother must have picked up on the mockery in Nancy's voice, for she was red-faced with fury. She let rip with a bark that would scrape the paint off a wall.

'I come from a people who have more learning in their shite than you have in your fuckin' big skull.' Nancy was winded by this outburst and she began to tug uneasily at the straps of her shopping bag.

'I was only——' she groaned feebly.

'You were only trying to make a show of me, you snobby bitch,' my mother butted in before Nancy could have her say. She was becoming stroppier by the minute and when she headed for Nancy with her hand raised up to clout her, I stepped out in front, grabbed her by the waist and, with all the strength of my eight-year-old persuasiveness, put a stop to her before she assaulted the other woman.

'Only for the boy I'd sweep the road with that hussy brush of hair on you,' she hissed at Nancy and the venom in it was as sharp as a wasp sting. I knew that my fiery, ill-tempered mother, who had vengeance in her eyes, would think nothing of doing Nancy an injury, so I was relieved when McFadden nudged her out of harm's way.

'By cripes, you're some fierce woman, Agnes, when you get going,' he said with a forced grin as he hauled the trembling Nancy up the steps and into the van, to get her supplies.

The nub of all this was that I vowed to myself, there and then, that I would learn to read and write so that we would not have to suffer this sort of public ridicule any more. Once I set my mind to it I grasped the basics of reading and writing readily enough. As if ducked in cold water, something inside me sprang to attention. For a month or two I was an attentive hush, a sponge absorbing the inky texts in my books. What was hitherto a mystery began to yield its meaning. Messy scrawls that looked like bird droppings, hairy caterpillars and the slime of snails revealed themselves to be recognisable syllables and identifiable words. I was amazed that the array of letters which they called the alphabet could be arranged in such endless combinations of shapes; signs that were decipherable and could be said, marks that held meaning inside them.

Soon I was attempting my own inky scribblings. I couldn't get over how a lush density of letters and a liaison of syllables became words and sentences. The delightful strangeness of it kept me enthralled. Diligent with concentration, I scribbled and scrawled my way through one copybook after another until I succeeded in writing a letter.

Inevitably that first letter was to my father. I can still see it, a big illegible squiggle written across two lined pages which I removed from the centre of my English copybook. Nothing of what I wrote in that letter comes to mind, only that it looked as if a very panicky bird had clawed its way over the pages. Despite its shaky hesitation, I can still remember the joy of shaping it, deciding what had to be said and choosing the right words (as far as my meagre word-hoard in English allowed) to say it.

Compared to the dull, tiresome writing exercises I had done at school this was a pleasurable undertaking which gave me a real charge of energy. After all, I was sending my father something uniquely my own.

PART TWO

Logic and sermons never convince.
The damp of the night drives deeper into the soul.

Walt Whitman

My mother was an inveterate traveller in the otherworld; a regular visitor to unearthly parts. She journeyed to places that were beyond the bounds of time, set foot in the outbacks of the fantastic, crossed the threshold into the inexplicable.

I was reared in a household that straddled two worlds; this world and the otherworld. My mother, who was illiterate, believed fervently in the fairies. She believed that another reality co-existed with ours, a hidden, supersensory domain inhabited by the *sí*, the fairy people. According to her, we were in and out of this world unbeknown to ourselves. She was anyway, but, unlike the rest of us, she was acutely conscious of these crossings and alert to the gravity of passing into their areas of activity.

'See the wispy green light floatin' yonder in thon field,' she would say anxiously as if we had stumbled upon something covert and dangerous. No matter how much I'd squint and peer I couldn't see that foreboding light that hovered over our lea.

'Where is it, Mammy? I can't see it.' I could see that she was a bit put out by my lack of preternatural vision.

'Where's your eyes, child, on your arse?'

I'd ignore her scoffs, and scan the far field with an even greater thoroughness but still that light eluded me.

'It's them movin'. Don't gawp!' Her body twitched nervously as if she were getting mild electric shocks. Then the moment of dread passed and she was back to her usual cheery self.

'They're out for an outin' in the light. I bet they're headin' up to Scaird for a wee dip in the hot springs.'

'Who?' I was so dim and dull-witted when challenged by my mother's odd and uncanny world.

'A heap of the Caor an Airgid ones. I know them rightly.' Caor an Airgid, a fairy place she often mentioned, lay on the far side of Errigal, somewhere in the vicinity of Sliabh Sneachta.

A globetrotter of the otherworld, familiar with its shape and size, my mother had no grasp whatsoever of the geography of this world. An atlas to her was more inscrutable than stone. After all, certain stones with their furry lichen tongues spoke to her, invited her into their roomy depths, gave her good-natured advice.

'That grey stone by the trees is saying there's a gale comin' from Gleann Tornáin,' she'd announce with irrefutable conviction. More often than not she was right. A howling storm would swoop from the east, striking fear into me for having doubts about her bizarre forewarnings.

Although she had been abroad, a migrant worker in Scotland with occasional stints in the Shetlands and the north of England, she had no sense of the sweep and stretch of these places, no notion of their position in relation to each other, no idea of them as geographic specifics on a map. Her overseas travels hadn't given her any grounding, whatsoever, in geography. Illiterate and unworldly, my hapless mother depended on other people to mind and steer her on journeys beyond her familiar locale. On her own she could make her way by foot or by bus to the nearby villages of Gortahork and Falcarragh. From time to time she sallied forth unaccompanied on the long thump and thud bus journey to her mother's house in Mín Doire na Slua, a townland in the outlying parish of the Rosses. If on the rare occasion she had to go to Letterkenny to attend the hospital there, she had to be chaperoned.

On the other hand she was inordinately informed about places that were off the map. She could tell you more about places that were out of this world than those that were in it. My mother's sense of geography was solely of the ineffable rather than of the actual. Her otherworldly peregrinations made a far greater impression on her than any of her worldly travels. For a woman who was naively simple about worldly affairs, she was amazingly *au fait* with the set-up and the goings-on of the otherworld. She could tell you that Scan was a grand principality of the *sí*, magnificently spread out in opulent splendour on the warm, lush plain between the river Eall and the hills of Agall. It took seven stiff, uphill nights, eastward from our home in Mín A Leá, to reach this dazzling kingdom that held sway over the vast arid lands of Donn an Domhain, the rich gold deposits of Pulc and the forbidden city of Ball na mBuacán where the ancient sages resided. 'Night', by the way, was the yardstick and the gauge by which she determined all distances to the beyond. ''Tis a lonesome wander in the dark,' she would say, 'where you have to tramp miles of night before you get there; a journey, you see, that's not fit for day.'

Likewise, her otherworldly place names sounded rather odd and curious and although they were Gaelic, they were distinctly unlike any of the names found commonly in our area. Béalard, Caor an Airgid, Bun na mBró, Tulc, Ruacan, Fán, Daol, Stron, Séad na Scéach, Idir Eatharthu, Dearg na gCorr. Anyway, those strange and spooky names gripped and thrilled my child's mind. As a wee boy, I was often hopping mad with my mother because she wouldn't let me accompany her on any of her out-of-this-world journeys. When I thought about Scan, that glitzy, far-off world, I felt in high spirits. It fired my imagination so much that I glowed with enthusiasm. I was dead set on seeing a place where the houses were made from gold, buffed to a fine lustrous sheen and thatched with the silk wings of gleaming blue birds of prey. I couldn't understand why she stubbornly refused to take me with her, especially when I gave her my solemn oath that I would dote on her every day and never, ever pester her, be rude or rough in her presence or bothersome in any way. I would whine and grumble, throw a tantrum or feign convulsions, but no ruse of mine ever succeeded in making her back down.

'Why can't I go?' My weepy pleas had no effect on her either.

'Thon there is no place for a child to go.' Her gruff firmness only made me more obstinate.

'Why?' All my pent-up disappointment came out in a screech.

'A wee scallywag like you can't go off gallivanting in the night.'

'We'll go by day.' I was not to be deterred.

'God, but aren't you the thran wee pest. Didn't I tell you yesterday that Scan is a faraway spot, deep in the black night where you don't let sleep next or near for fear of losing your way? You'd conk out like a wee candle stub in a breeze and that would be the last of you.'

I knew that it was crucial not to give way to sleep on these perilous journeys; otherwise, you put your life in jeopardy. You had to remain awake and alert at all times. If you allowed yourself to be overcome by sleep, you would be, as my mother often impressed upon me, 'gobbled up in a wild swirl of black'. I knew right well that it would be a staggering feat for me not to yield to sleep, but I was so fixated on seeing the pomp and the parades and the razzle-dazzle of Scan that I would risk anything to go there. No matter how much of a fuss I made she was adamant that I wasn't going to Scan or indeed to any of the other mystifying places that she frequented. For a long time I clung earnestly to the hope that one day she would relent and I'd see that fantabulous realm that lay serenely between the river Eall and the hills of Agall. I never did.

Usually she went off without warning. While washing clothes or brushing the floor or baking bread she would suddenly become distracted, skew her head to one side and peer into some shadowy beyond.

'I'll have to be off to Caor an Airgid. They're calling me.'

'Why, Mammy?'

'They're having bother with a baby they took from the west. They need a wet nurse for a wee while.'

She would drop whatever she was doing and straight away take herself off to bed. Curled up, she lay there for two or three hours in a drowse, her breathing odd and patchy. After some time she would wake up, a little off colour perhaps, with a look of bewilderment on her face as if the ordeal of the journey had unnerved her. It distressed her when they took a baby from some unsuspecting mother and she was called upon to calm and comfort it in its unfamiliar setting and ease it into its otherworldly upbringing. 'I pity that poor woman in faraway Galway who lost her baby. And a lovely brawny boy it is. I was sore troubled leaving it behind me.'

She was genuinely upset by their ruthless kidnappings, but at the same time she would never condemn them outright. They were quite intolerable, particularly the *sí* of Caor an Airgid. They were a scheming, devious lot and appallingly nasty if you meddled, even unwittingly, in their affairs or intruded in any way upon their haunts. They would psych you out, terrorise your household, maim your cattle. They were a dab hand at making life a living nightmare for anyone who antagonised them. In fact, I often saw her wince when someone spoke scathingly of them. 'The wee scoundrels,' she would say, soothingly, 'sure, there's no harm in their capers.'

She knew that it was a risk to provoke or slag them off in any way. After all, she had a close relationship with them, but a cautious one. They were often mean and nasty and easily offended.

'They were in a terrible huff last night over a man in the Rosses who's buildin' a house on a route they use. The scowls of them would blacken a summer's day. He's a goner, that man, so he is, with the grudge they have against him.'

There was always mischief and skulduggery going on in those fairy settlements, especially in Caor an Airgid. I knew from my mother that they took strong, sturdy newborn babies and replaced them with their own scrawny weaklings. They were deadly abductors. According to my mother the *sí* of Caor an Airgid were remote descendants of Aingle an Díomais – the arrogant angels who became so overbearing and bossy that the Almighty himself had no option but to dispossess them of their divine rights and have them flung into the squalid pit of the netherworld, the woeful abode of mortals. Sullied and godforsaken, they took up residence in out-of-the-way places, lonesome glens and solitary groves.

'No wonder they're so grumpy,' my mother would say, 'the poor wee souls have lost so much.'

'These scorned angels,' she said, 'will only be allowed back into heaven if on the Day of Judgment they can show a trickle of red blood in their veins.'

'Don't angels have blood in their veins?' I would query, fascinated by the make-up of these elemental beings.

'Not a smidgen of red blood in that airy lot. They have a dazzle of white that runs in them like soapy water. They're not hefty sorts like us at all. They can shift about easily like wee sudsy clouds.'

This streak of red blood in their veins would be evidence that they had waived their divinity and had yielded to the chastening shame of impermanency. This, they believed, would appease the Almighty so that whatever bad blood remained between them could be patched up and put to rights. Then, and only then, would they be restored to the resplendence of their former glory. This was why they were forever stealing mortal babies so that they could keep replenishing the tribe's stock of red blood.

Although they survived for hundreds of years, they too, like us, had to endure the agony of death. Despite their apparent perishability, my mother believed that they had the power to reanimate themselves after death.

'Like puffin' up a balloon, they can fill a dead body with some kind of strange air. Pump it up like and in no time at all the corpse is breathin' like me or you.' Some of them, she told me, the more exalted ones, usually had no desire to be reinstated in their former bodies. They passed on to a loftier level of existence, she said.

I envied these elemental beings their flair to fade, melt away and evaporate like steam off a boiling kettle or like drifting smoke dissolving in the sky. I wanted their lightsome mobility, their knack to take to the air and get to a place in two ticks. I yearned for their soft, vaporous flimsiness that defied gravity. I longed for their sleek, aerodynamic grace. Thinking about them, I felt so coarse, so corpulent, so cooped up in weighty flesh. I resented being so earthbound. I wanted to shed all the shoddy bulk that prevented me from flying. I craved to be airborne. What fun it would be to whoosh across fields, to soar about hills, to hover over lakes, to glide and swoop like a hawk, to dip and curve like a swallow.

Apparently they didn't look anything at all like the corny pictures of fairies in my English storybook.

'That's all balderdash. They look no more like that than the man in the moon.'

'What do they look like, Mammy?'

'They're scraggy wee things, kinda gawky with yellow skin like a September cornfield but they can hoodwink you rightly and take on any shape. There's a wicked sour smell off them like butter going bad. A heap of them, the poor wee things, suffer badly from boils and sores. That's why they're the devil for *báchrán*.'

Báchrán, or bogbean, is a medicinal plant that grows in bog holes. In the past, people pulled up this soggy root from the bog, usually in March, boiled it in water, and drank the bitter juice, believing that it cleansed the blood. My father was a great believer in *báchrán* and every spring dug it up and boiled it. Although it was tasteless, I always felt my skin glow after drinking a cup of his dark bog brew.

She was adamant about one thing: she never took any of their food or drinks, however much they cajoled her with their fancy fare. She declined all that they offered politely but firmly. 'Not a bite to eat nor a sup to drink would I let near me for fear of them getting a right hold of me,' she often told me.

She often mentioned Béalard. It was a grim, craggy place, 'the length of a Samhain's night away'. It was an enclave of seedy hillbilly *sí*, coarse cattle rustlers who seized the priceless white, red-eared cows of their more genteel fairy neighbours in the bordering areas of Tulc, Ruacan and Fán. Her bizarre wayfaring exploits were always told in a coherent, clear-headed manner.

'The wee scoundrels, I see them come tearin' down the big brae at Rua in a wild whack of wind for to lift cattle in Tulc. Come on, me girl, I say to meself, quick, I'll take the short cut around Daol, up Stron and over the rampart to Tulc to tell them what's whirlin' down on them fast. Out thon in the open I was tinglin' wi' the cold but by the time I got to Tulc – and I was there, mind you, right smart – the sweat was puffin' off me. I told them I didn't want to be meddlin' in their business – they're snooty enough sometimes about things like that, you know. But the thievin' boyos of Béalard were sneakin' down on them fast to snatch their cows and they'd have sore trouble keepin' them out if they weren't waitin' prepared. Like a flash they were buckled up and rigged out for fightin'. When the Béalards came snoopin' in expectin' nothing they got a terrible trouncin'. In no time at all the scuffle was over and they were headin' back up the hill, the wee scamps, howlin' something fierce and with no whit of a cow. They were right thankful to me at Tulc. After that, they have great feelin' for me and they say there'll never be a want on us.'

Every now and then she went to a place called Idir Eatharthu, The Place In Between, sited underneath a boggy hollow some-where in that hilly stretch between Dunlewey and Doohery. It was an intriguing place because it was entirely threshold, a place that was neither inside nor outside, neither entrance nor exit. As a child I wondered about its pure outright wackiness. A place that was wholly doorway, yet was neither the way in nor the way out, left me baffled. The more I tried to think it out the more bewildering it became. My mother, when I pressed her to be more explicit, only made matters worse by her enigmatic reply.

'There's places west of midnight where the roots of your hair would go as white as the winter moon shinin' on a gravestone.'

Her evasiveness drove me up the wall. I craved for an orderly explanation, for something lucid and logical that would make this abstract space a more intelligible place for me. At the time, I was not at all amenable to the notion of a place being as indefinite as Idir Eatharthu.

'Don't be daft,' she would say, weary of my tiresome questions. 'Some places are nowhere and everywhere. They're there on the edge of nothin'.'

'What's nothing?' I would fire at her. I felt she was trying to fudge me off. She would stand there and glare at me.

''Tis no wonder I have a scowl on me as long as a wet Sunday.

95

You'll have me mental, child, if you don't stop your gab. There's no place in nothin' no more than there's breath in a dead body. I tell you, it's a *lom* in the black. Aye, indeed, an awful *lom.*'

'Why do you go to Idir Eatharthu?'

'Because I have to feed the *nathair breac.*'

The *nathair breac* was a hideous, foul-smelling, coppery-brown serpent coiled around Crann an Domhan, or the world tree, an enormous nut-bearing evergreen that shed its fruit every hour and grew it again instantly. This vile reptile that stank, she said, 'so bad that it would sicken the guts of a parish priest' had to be fed every once in a while with uniquely nutritious milk from a herd of fair, light-yellow milch cows that grazed the rich grasslands of Séad na Scéach. From time to time it was her lot to feed the serpent. She had to carry two frothy buckets of milk across the mile-long springy plank that spanned the chasm between Séad na Scéach and Idir Eatharthu without spilling a drop of the ambrosial cream. She would place the two milk pails warily at the foot of the tree and withdraw to a safe distance until the loathsome *nathair* had supped the milk and slithered back up the tree.

When my mother complained of 'fire in her head', I knew that she was about to undertake one of her risky journeys to Dearg na gCorr. I dreaded those journeys, especially the initiatory hysterics; the feverish onset of whatever it was that came upon her. Over a period of five or six weeks, she would visibly wane before my eyes. It was shocking to see her undergo such an appalling change. From being a stout, sturdy woman she would suddenly lose all that plump, pink fleshiness, and become a gaunt and scrawny starveling.

She usually stayed in bed or else slumped by the fireside and sobbed out a raving tumult of sounds. I could never make out what she said. Her words, if those rasps and shrieks she let out were words and not some archaic babble, were like disembowelled vowels, discordant consonants that had yet to be coaxed into meaning. As she became more manic the sounds became noticeably more throaty; guttural sighs, low growling moans, croaky grunts that heaved up from deep inside her.

At this point she would feverishly poke the ashes on the open hearth with the tongs and sketch out a rough pattern of circles and spirals, disc-shaped swirls and notched lines, shapes that looked like a runic alphabet, as if she were sending coded messages to the beyond. I don't know what these graphic configurations meant to her or whether they were just distractions; nervous scrapings, jittery drawings to ease the agitation in her head. As a child I didn't pay much attention to them. They were, I thought, some crazed thing she did when she was sick in the head. When the sounds she made grew exuberantly lush, much like the sweet cooing chants she sang while milking the cow, I knew that she was on her way back to us.

After five or six weeks of shrivelling up and shrinking into herself, she would emerge one morning, a little unsteady on her feet as if still dazed and fatigued from her long exacting journey, but otherwise in good shape.

'I was in Dearg na gCorr for a few weeks,' she would claim timidly, looking around a woefully messy kitchen that had gone mostly untended for weeks.

Dearg na gCorr was an otherworldly domain situated seven nights west of Errigal. It was a place inhabited by a race of long-limbed beings, powerful enchanters who practised *draíocht na gcorr*, crane wizardry, to preserve and purify the luminous realm that they inhabited. This entailed standing rigidly on one leg for three days in a shimmering river, closing one eye and chanting. They survived on a heady mix of rare fungi and red berries, pulverised into a fine crimson powder which gave them an easy facility to change shape and become bird or beast or an amorphous assemblage of both which my mother referred to as *sceith frog na n-eiteog*, winged frogspawn. They carried this precious powder at all times in a little pouch called *bolg an tsolais* that glowed bright as a will-o'-the-wisp in the dark.

The benign dwellers of Dearg na gCorr, who were not subject to death, believed that only a *duine daonna*, a mortal, could imbue the magic blend with maximum potency. Thus my mother was called upon to gather the revered ingredients – the wild fungi and the red berries – which grew abundantly in a holy grove on a hilltop. She then had to grind them separately with a silver pestle. A *fear feasa*, a sage, conducted the final sacred fusion amidst great liturgical splendour on Inis Ór na gCorr, the Golden Island of the Cranes, an incandescent island in the sky used for such ceremonial purposes and propped up by a flock of gigantic golden-plumed cranes.

The inhabitants of Dearg na gCorr were not, according to my mother, of the fairy kind. They were a race of superior beings who had sealed themselves off from a calamitous world ages and ages ago. With a daily dose of *caor na mbéacán*, as my mother referred to their divine opiate of mushrooms and berries, these pharmaceutically audacious beings lived an unending life of bliss in their ethereal hideaway. My mother had to undergo a period of purification before she could pass into their bright, unblemished haven of light. She was more guarded about the goings-on of Dearg na gCorr than she was about any of the other esoteric destinations on her hectic itinerary.

'I can't be telling about it. It's a *dearg rún*,' (literally, a red secret) she would yell at me, fed up with my prying questions. But every once in a while I managed to cajole her with my cherubic blandishments and she would grudgingly offer a little glimpse of the shrouded Dearg na gCorr.

'How do they clean you up, Mammy, before you get in to Dearg na gCorr?'

'They swaddle me up in some type of shinin' tin and bundle me into this steamin' gadget. I'm in there 'til I'm as soggy as a wet sod. It gives me a good scourin', mind you, from the inside out. When I'm shinin' like a new shillin', I'm let go to pick the wild stuff.'

Once when I asked her how she got to Dearg na gCorr she told me she travelled there by blue. 'I got a birl from blue,' she said matter-of-factly. With the rational, no-nonsense approach the primary school was instilling in me I found this rather far-fetched and unfeasible.

'But Mammy, you can't travel on a colour. It just can't be done,' I said, vehemently denying even the possibility of it. And she, without showing the slightest doubt or unease, said, 'If you're stuck in the night, child, you'll take a lift from anything that is passing by.'

Madge is an artist and she lives away out in Prochlais. The grey
bulk of Achla Mór rears its horsey head to the sky across the valley
from her house. Her gleaming white cottage on a craggy rise is
sited between a fairy wood and a dark bog lake. It's a summer's
day and my mother and I are visiting her. We took the short cut
across the ridge, a mile or so of a tramp through dry, stumpy
heather, to bring her a clutch of duck eggs for hatching.

The frail tendrils of woodbine that cling to the stone wall of
her yard are as delicate as the fingers of a wee girl trying to climb
up the wall and see what is on the other side. She is also like that,
I think, full of a lively curiosity about things. She stands in the
doorway, a stout woman in a green floral dress, and enthuses
about the lilies that are blooming in her small plot of flowers.

'Look at them lilies! Aren't they're pretty?'

My mother and I gaze at them with delight. They are velvety
white tongues humming with bees.

'Come on in for a wee drop of tea,' she says in a soft, unhurried
voice, motioning us into her kitchen. A big red geranium on the
table fills the place with a sharp, tangy scent. I notice a picture of
a boldly drawn Errigal hanging on the wall by the window,
coloured in what looks like cigarette foil silver. The sky above it
is a pink glisten of clouds and the bottom veers off into a purple
fleck of bog.

'Do you recognise that mountain?' she asks me. It's more a
tactic to get me talking, I realise, than a question.

'That's Errigal,' I say.

'I did that one last week. It's a damn hard mountain to catch.'

'Why?' I ventured, forgetting my shyness.

'Because it keeps changing its face. With every shift of light it gets a new one. Errigal has more faces on it than a crowd at a Celtic football match.'

She peers at me with an inquisitive eye and asks, 'What do you see in this Errigal?'

I look down at the floor, unsure of what to say. 'It's like a . . . silver jug with a . . . a piece of pink soap on top of it,' I stammer out at last.

She laughs at that and says to my mother, 'Agnes, that boy has an eye.'

'Aye, like meself, he sees what's not there more than he sees what's there,' my mother says as she removes the duck eggs from her shopping bag and places them carefully in a deep, yellow bowl on the dresser.

'I hope these hatching eggs will be lucky for you, Madge. You've got great scope here for ducks with the water and all beside you.'

'It's grand, Agnes, except that the fox is always on the prowl. Yesterday, he nabbed another of my hens.'

I sit by the set-in bed and stroke a small tawny cat that purrs contentedly on a tasselled cushion at my feet while the two women natter away. Madge wets the tea in a bulbously fancy teapot, lets it draw and then pours it gracefully into dainty blue cups.

'I bought this willow-pattern tea set at a sale in Glasgow,' she tells my mother. She hands me a cup. It's scalding hot. I wince with pain and the cup slips through my sliddery fingers and cracks into little shimmering flickers of delph on the flagstoned floor. My heart is pumping hard with fright. This is my first time in her house and I've smashed her precious tea cup.

'You're a wee clouster, so you are,' my mother says,

reprimanding me. I want to get away from what I've done. I rush out the door and scramble up the hill behind the house, sobbing.

'Come down here, you wee scrunt and don't be actin' the maggot,' my mother shouts up at me. Dolly, Madge's old shaggy donkey, is munching wisps of grass beside me. Her face looks sad and mournful like the cheerless face of Jesus in the Stations of the Cross. I look away and hear the drone of bees in the heather. It's like the dull hum of penitents in the church when they murmur their prayers after confession. It rankles in my ear. I get a tightening in the pit of my stomach when I see my mother and Madge clambering up the slope to where I'm sitting.

'I'm sorry, Madge, I'm sorry,' I cry out in gulping sobs.

'It's alright, you've only broken a silly wee cup, dear.' Her voice is kind and tender. She pats my flushed cheeks and smooths back my tangle of sweaty curls. Mother takes my hand and coaxes me down the brae. Back in the kitchen, Madge takes out a flat tin box full of a glossy, wet mess of colours and a thick leaf of sheeny paper.

'I'm going to paint a wee picture of Prochlais for you,' she says, grinning at me with a ready enthusiasm. I sit at the table beside her and watch her work. She holds a slender brush in her hand, daubs it in her box of wet paints and stains the paper with a dribble of colour. A splodge of brown, a dash of blue, a smear of grey, a glob of green and there is Prochlais gleaming at me in a wash of colours. It's all there, the lake, the bog, the scatter of houses, the stony hulk of a mountain. It's the first time I witness an artist at work. It fills me with wonderment to see her sitting at the table rapt in her painting like a saint praying or like the visionary I saw in the church magazine, his face aglow with whatever he was seeing. Perhaps she too is a miracle worker. If she can put a landscape together so effortlessly, I think to myself, maybe she can put the shattered cup together again. I gaze around her cool, delph-bright kitchen and feel better about myself.

'A wee view of Prochlais for yourself. I hope you like it,' she said and handed me the finished picture. Her voice is a sweet curl of vine that trails itself around me and cheers me up. I take the picture in my hand and peer at it. Up close it looks like a gloopy muddle of colours but when I hold it out at arm's length I see Prochlais plain as day.

'It's lovely, Madge.' I beam up at her reassuringly. Then on a sudden impulse I hug her. She laughs out loud and places a big dollop of a kiss on my cheek. She has moist, shiny eyes that ooze with light like the dark, sweet syrup that my mother spreads on my bread sometimes.

'It's the first time I got a hug for one of my pictures but I hope it's not the last one,' she confides in me, then grins, and with her fingers, gently tweeks my cheek.

After we say our goodbyes she stands at the corner of her sunlit house and I keep waving to her until we round a bend in the road.

Below us, the fairy wood of Prochlais, a rambling tangle of ash, hazel and sally slopes down to the Sweeneys' farm. It is a screen of green that covers one side of the hill. As always it is eerily quiet. Even the birds, it seems to me, have kept away from it. Maybe they too are fearful of disturbing its green silence. The wood was 'uasal', enchanted, and none of the locals would cut down a tree in it nor would they pick its nuts and berries or gather firewood there for fear of vexing the wee folk. My mother told me that they didn't live there, it was just a way in, an opening to their world.

It occurred to me as we were passing that the fairies were good to Madge and maybe even gave her a helping hand with her painting. I broached this with my mother.

'They don't do her any bad, that's for sure,' she answered with a wry smile. 'Madge keeps a good eye on their property and they keep an eye on her. Anyway, she has the eye for painting.'

'Maybe the fairies gave her a magical eye, Mammy, so that she can see more colour than anybody else.' I was holding her Prochlais in my hand. It was interesting to see both of them at the same time, the painted Prochlais and the actual Prochlais. It was clear that Madge saw a more delicate range of colours than what was visible to me. She saw tints of red and hints of yellow where I saw nothing but a murky bog brown. Until that day I thought of Prochlais as a place shadowed by mountains, stark and scant of light. Madge opened my eyes to a Prochlais that was a shock of startling colours.

'I know a woman who got a song off the *síogaí*,' my mother said as we veered off the road and cut across the bog. 'And a fiddler who got the gift of a tune. I never heard word of them meddling with paints, but who knows what the new breed will be like.'

Coming down by Loch an Ghainimh we came across a dead sheep, a spongy mass of rotting flesh lying in the heather. There was a swirl of flies buzzing around the stink and when I looked closer I saw a white glisten of maggots moving in the mire. Normally such a sight would sicken me but that evening I made little of it. I was so enthralled by my picture that a smelly sheep wasn't going to bother me.

When I got home I found an old battered frame in the barn with a fading holy picture in it. I took the picture out, polished up the frame as best I could and fitted Prochlais into it. Unbeknownst to myself I was becoming a devotee of art rather than of religion. I placed the framed picture on the mantelpiece in our bedroom right between two brown china dogs.

As it happened that was my first and only contact with Madge. Soon after that she sold out, left Prochlais and went to live in faraway Ramelton. My father pointed it out on the map and said it would take the best part of a day to get there by bus. On the map it was just a dot, a speck of black on the wiggly blue of Lough Swilly. 'She's had enough of them lonely hills. Now she wants to make a life for herself down there by the sea,' was how my mother explained her going away. I was sad when she left. Without her Prochlais would be a lonelier place.

However, I had her picture and when I looked at it I saw a Prochlais where earth and sky clasped each other in a hug of light. That lifted my spirits.

I would sit sometimes on the rise above our house and watch the lingering touch of sunlight on the curve of a cloud and imagine that Madge was watching the same thing in Ramelton.

Christmas Day. I got up at first light, crept out of bed, cautiously, without stirring Mammy and Daddy. Although ten, I still slept in their bed. Wedged cosily between the two of them, I felt safe; on my own I would be afraid that some ghostly hand would lay hold of me in the dark. The wee hours of the night, I knew from Mammy, were full of spooky goings-on. While one world rested, she said, another world took over. There was a chill air in the room. On stockinged feet I tiptoed across the hard stone floor to where my clothes hung over a chair by the wardrobe. A cold draught from somewhere made me gasp. I pulled on my clothes in a hurry and slipped down to the kitchen. In the window, a Christmas candle, burnt down to a messy stub, caught my eye as I pulled open the curtains on a bright, frosty dawn. A shock of raw light hit my eyes. I blinked.

Jutting up from its splodge of wax, the candle stump looked like my own wee mickey when it got stiff in the morning. At first this hardening left me bewildered, until I read in a book that it was a part of growing up and becoming a man. But at this very moment I didn't want to be a man, because Santa didn't come to grown-ups. The previous night I had hung up my stocking on our sooty crane. Ours was an open fire, and when I peeked up the wide chimney to make sure it wasn't blocked I saw a wink of lights in the sky and knew that Santa was on his way.

A few days before, my father had gone to Falcarragh and bought 'The Christmas'. He was down to his last pound, he said, and we would have to do with whatever he had the money for. He came back with a small iced cake, jelly and custard, three shiny red apples, two bars of Cadbury's chocolate and a bottle of gassy lemonade for me; two ounces of plug tobacco and a baby Power's for himself; and twenty Sweet Afton for Mammy, her favourite fags.

That year he wasn't able to go to Scotland because Mammy took sick and had to be looked after. She stumbled about the house like a drunk, or else drowsed in bed for days on end. She'd lost her bearings, she told us, coming back from the otherworld on nights when she'd had to take long slogs across bogs full of sucking holes. Coming up to Christmas she improved, and now she was in fine fettle. Together we whitewashed the kitchen and cheered it up with sprigs of red-berried holly. Daddy killed a big, plump rooster. I watched him do it. One swift twist to the neck, it flapped limply in his grip and died. Mammy and myself plucked it clean, its itchy fluff tickling our faces and making us laugh. Daddy was short on cash and couldn't spare the price of toys. Santa was sure to know this, because he was wise. Strangely enough, it was those with the wherewithal to buy whatever they fancied that got the biggest and best gifts from him. I knew that, but shoved it to the back of my mind as I apprehended the chimney crane with a thumping heart. There was my stocking, hanging as I had left it. A streak of soot oozed down its side – and Jesus, Mary and Joseph, I couldn't believe it – there was nothing in it. Frantically, I searched round the kitchen, thinking he had hidden my presents somewhere just to get me into a wee bit of a dither. I found nothing at all. Santa had left me bugger all. On the table there was a wee packet with 'To Charlie *beag* from Mammy and Daddy' written on it. Wrapped up clumsily in brown paper, it contained a poke of liquorice allsorts and four copper pennies. I was sure Santa would leave me some toy soldiers, as well as a cowboy outfit, maybe, or even a middling-sized gun. But no, he'd left me damn all.

I rushed up to the room, nudged my father awake and, sobbing loudly, told him that Santa hadn't left me anything. He sat up in bed and shook his head grimly. Wearing only a thin, short-sleeved simmit, he shivered, clasped his arms around himself and groaned. He had long, strong arms, and seeing them strapped around him like this with their thick, corded sinews pulled taut made me think he was roped up and trapped. He looked at me and grimaced. I knew that whatever he was going to say weighed heavily on him.

'We never know, *a chroí*, when or where the shoe will pinch us,' he began, looking down at the floor where his old working-boots stood by the bedside. They had the wrinkled, caked-hard look of dried cowshite. Recently I had heard him complain that the left one was rubbing him. 'But with a bit of luck,' he said, regarding me with a curious smile, 'it'll soften up and, who knows, it might even stretch out a bit.' And then, as if he wanted it over and done with, he hurried out the words and told me that there was no Santa, that it was the mammies and daddies who filled up the stockings, that he was so broke that Christmas that he couldn't afford to buy me any toys. We barely had enough, he said, to buy a wee bit of extra food.

We would survive, he said, and some day life would be brighter and better for all of us. I could see tears filling his eyes, but he resolutely held back the flow by shutting them tight. I lost myself in a patch of light that came through a chink in the curtains and dallied around his old boots.

'You know, the blow that doesn't kill you usually strengthens you,' I heard him say as he patted my back reassuringly.

I wasn't entirely surprised that there was no Santa. I had heard rumours at school, but conveniently paid no attention to them. What really shocked me was the pain on my father's face as he spoke. Mammy roused herself up out of the blankets. I could hear her sob into her pillow when Daddy was talking, but now she was putting on a cheery face.

'Themselves,' she said cheerily, meaning the fairies, 'gave me a wee nod just now. You'll be rolling about in money some day, they told me, don't you worry.'

She ran her hand through her thick brown hair, loosening it up. It flowed down her back like a big swoosh of dropping pennies. She was so pretty, now that she was getting a little colour back in her cheeks and putting on flesh again after her illness.

A picture of God, bearded and jovial like Santa, surrounded by beefy wee angels, hung in a corner by the wardrobe. If Santa was a fraud, I wondered, was God also a hoax? I had a feeling that I was growing, that the low timber ceiling in the room was in my way. Now that Santa wasn't coming any more, I must be a grown-up.

While Mammy and Daddy were getting up, I went to the kitchen door, unlatched it and walked out into a hard, frosty glitter. The bars on a rickety gate opposite the house were trimmed with sparkling crystals. The cattle tracks by the cow byre were iced ruts and glistened. It was lovely to scrunch through the snow. Our steep lane where water seeped down from the road was now a slippery bottle of ice. It was a morning full of promise.

I was now twelve years old. At the primary school, I was in the authoritarian care of the master, who taught the senior pupils. He was a severe, unsmiling man entirely focused on getting his students through the scholarship hoops. He worked tirelessly to achieve this, year in, year out, and never once faltered in his determination. Every year a batch of his students passed with flying colours and adoring parents praised him lavishly. He was on a mission to get the brightest children in his care into furthering their education so that they would get ahead in life and into secure, pensionable jobs and not have to emigrate. But for that push, that head start, many people in our area would not have gone on to better themselves in a whole range of professions. I wasn't brainy enough and showed no flair for arithmetic, which at the time was the real test in rating intelligence, and had no aptitude to trot out the facts that were given me in a neat, coherent order; and so was not considered fit to sit for the exams. I kept my head down and took the occasional beating. These punishments were inescapable, almost obligatory so as not to be singled out as a teacher's pet. Only once, contrary to my intentions, was I foolhardy enough to show a little enthusiasm, a wee gleam of originality, and got the rap for it. I should have known better.

It happened like this. For our homework we were ordered to write an essay, 'The Day I Went Fishing'. Our essay had to be strictly formulaic: no offhanded oddness, no curious ideas, no quirks of language were encouraged. Clear, legible penmanship, good spelling and a page or two of bland itemising – 'I got up at eight o'clock in the morning. I put on my clothes. I said my prayers. I ate my breakfast' – was the sort of thing that was required. At the time I was reading Lewis Carroll's *Through the Looking Glass*, which my father had bought for me in Glasgow. I was so captivated by his askew, topsy-turvy world that I wanted to try out a bit of my own Humpty-Dumptyism. I don't know what came over me to dare such a risky essay, but when I finished it I felt exhilarated by its wonky vision.

The Day I Went Fishing
I got up at the break of dreams. It was dawn o'clock. I put on my black prayers and said my morning trousers. I came down the breakfast and ate a big slice of home-baked stairs. Then I went up to the fish. It was full of lakes. I caught one big brown one and took it home. My mother said, 'Good boy, we will boil this lake for tea and I will peel a few stones to go with it.' She poured a little daylight into a glass when I told her that I was thirsty. 'Would you like a light snack?' she asked. She buttered a slice of stairs with a bit of sun. It tasted even better than my favourite food which was mashed moon and a wee scallion of star with a drop of hot night. Then I woke up and went back to sleep.

In the morning we lined up in front of the master's desk while he read and corrected our written homework. He gave each essay a thorough going-over, sifting through the grammar, spelling and punctuation. No doubtful tense, no rogue capital, no miscreant comma, no lapse in sense went unnoticed. It was pounced upon and clamped in corrective red. Occasionally a word of praise was granted, but mostly you got your copybook back with a good scowling.

It was a hot, fusty morning in May. As I stood in line I could hear a rumble of thunder tumbling about somewhere beyond

Errigal. It was so stuffy in the classroom you could almost touch the heat. Like a presence, it quivered in our midst, unseen but solidly there. The May altar in the corner, decked with wild flowers in jam jars, gave off a weedy stench. When my turn came I stood at the master's desk and watched him read, head bowed, pen held at the ready to interrogate. The parting at the side of his head was prissy and straight, like a ruler. Everything about him was neat, careful, exact; his fussy nails, his gleaming shoes, his Brylcreemed hair, slicked back in an orderly wave. Even the hair that sprouted on his hands from knuckles to cuffs looked controlled.

Whatever the quirky nature of my composition, that morning I was quietly confident that my handwriting was good and that my spellings were correct. He read it through without one touch of the pen; then he raised his head, and, regarding me with glowering eyes, breathed out a snort of disapproval.

'What kind of daftness is this?' he yelled.

'It's an essay, sir,' I said without conviction.

'An essay?' he snarled. He shook his head and a coiled loop of hair sprung out and hung dangerously over his brow. He licked his lips, a loud moist slurp; that always indicated that he was in a rage.

'It's nonsense,' and before I could say anything he struck me across the face in one-two, one-two, quick, stinging slaps that made my cheeks burn. I could hardly breathe. Through the window I could see a patch of heavy sky, thick as clotted milk. I gulped for air.

'In all my days of teaching I have never got such drivel handed up to me,' he raged, and flung the copybook back at me. 'And another thing,' he spat out with aloof contempt, 'sure there's no stairs in your house.'

I crept back to my desk, seething with anger. In that breathless room I was about to explode. A roll of thunder ripped across the sky, and suddenly rain slashed down. I turned towards the master, tears welling up in my eyes, and hissed at him silently, 'Fuck you! Fuck you!'

At school, learning was not a graceful pursuit of knowledge but a ruthless head-plunge into a pit of facts. Everything was beaten into us. It wasn't entirely the teachers' fault. They themselves were the victims of a cruel and brutal schooling and, as is often the case with victimisation, they perpetuated and passed on with the same rigour the pain that was inflicted on them. Declensions and set expressions; formulas and fractions; tables, totals and tenses; lists, rules and litanies. It was a fact-based curriculum, a syllabus of algebraic tediousness that did not encourage creativity. Knowledge was no more than factual cleverness. It was all tot up, parse, count, figure out, calculate, and it bored me. I had no head for the sort of witless conundrums that we were asked to solve. 'A shopkeeper put £1 15s 6d in small change into his till in the morning. During the day he took 32s out of the till to pay a bill. How much did he take in for the day if there was £12 8s 9d in the till at closing time?' Unless I cogged the right answer off somebody who was good at reasoning out these shopkeeping enigmas, I was beaten, but more painful by far was to be berated in public. The master, who had a brilliant mind for numerical trivia, got so exasperated with me one day for not attempting any of the meticulously thought-out shopkeeping 'sums' that he had set for us that he made me stand on top of the desk and face the window.

'What do you see through that window?' He paused and I could hear him snigger. 'If it's in you to see anything.' Seeing was something I was good at, but I only gave him a glimpse of the obvious.

'I see Máire Rua's house hidden in the trees.'

'How can you see it if it's hidden?' he remarked drily.

'Because I know it's there, sir . . .'

He raised his eyes to heaven in a show of despair.

'What else do you see that's not there?'

'Smoke from the chimneys of Fana Bhuí fading away.'

He gave me a raw, hard look. I didn't know where this questioning was leading to, but I got the impression that it wasn't going his way.

'Beyond Fana Bhuí what do you see?'

'The road that takes you out of it, sir.'

He gave the tilted globe in the window a few angry whirls as if trying to straighten out this nonsensical world that I was spinning around him, but in doing so unsteadied it so much that it toppled over.

'Where does that road lead us?' he said, settling the globe back in the window and pointing to a white streak of gravel in the distance.

'That depends where you're going, sir.'

'You're not going any place,' he smirked. 'Where would a fellow who can't do a simple sum be going?'

I just shrugged. He was simmering on a slow-burning fire of anger and I didn't want to add any more fuel to it. A glisten of sweat appeared on his forehead just below the hairline.

'What hill do you see in front of you?' he said, regarding me with a fierce, unnerving look. I tried to collect my thoughts and see what he was seeing.

'The hills of Keeldrum,' I ventured.

'What's grazing on them?' At that moment a woolly cloud hovered over them.

'There's a big white cloud grazing on them now.'

'For God's sake, clouds don't graze,' he said irritably.

He was staring at me, trying to figure out whether I was genuinely half-witted or just fooling him.

'What has four legs, wool, goes mea-mea and grazes the hills?' he said in a clownish manner, as if addressing a dimwit. I had some inkling of where he was leading me, but I wasn't going to give him the easy satisfaction of spelling it out.

'A goat, sir,' I said, giving him a timid smile, knowing full well that nobody in the vicinity kept a goat.

'Goat!' he exclaimed in a flash of anger. 'Where in the name of sweet Jesus do you see a goat over there?'

'I just made it up, sir.'

His face was shiny and red. He loosened his carefully knotted tie before delivering himself.

'I'm giving you one last chance. What grass-eating animal with thick white wool and a name for being stupid . . .'

'A sheep, sir,' I chimed in to get him out of his agony.

'Exactly!' He nodded vigorously. 'Exactly. And do you know something?' He paused to give me a disapproving look. 'You'd be as well off out on that hill, grazing, because you have about as much brains as the stupidest of them sheep.'

The school had windows, but, looking back on it now, it seems to me that no light got in to brighten the grim, dispiriting rooms where we sat in fear. The only vivid things in those dim classrooms were the potted geraniums in the windows and the richly coloured maps on the walls. That blaze of red and the glow of faraway places always heartened me up a little when the going got tough.

I was lucky in that my parents had no aggressive social

ambitions for me. My mother couldn't have cared less if I never went to school. She was tuned in to an otherworldly wisdom way beyond the narrow confines of the ABC.

My father wanted me to have an education so that I would have a choice in life; a chance to be fully myself in whatever I opted to do.

'Education is a wee key,' he would say. 'Aye, boy, it gives you the right to go inside your head and open up them rooms that you didn't know were there. Education, you see, gives you a bit of headroom to move about in.'

Unlike some parents who set their sights, hard and fast, on a son becoming a priest or a daughter becoming a teacher, my father had no choosy expectations for me. Being a success with myself was, I think, what he hoped the most for me; in other words, a genuine desire to see me happy.

He was kicking about on his own in the rough field by the lake; a boy my age, I guessed, twelve, maybe thirteen; long in the leg with a pale, beaky face. His black trousers hung low on his hips and were kept up by a red knotty belt with a buckle which flared when the sun caught it. I watched him run with the ball, dodge and dribble, then turn with a deft swivel of the hips and lob it between the two stones which acted as goalposts. I stepped out from behind the thick growth of whins where I was jouking and approached him.

'Ah'm Jimmy. Ah'm fae Glasgow,' he said, tossing the ball to me invitingly. 'Are ye oan for a kick aboot?'

I stood, fidgeting with the ball, trying to make sense of what he was saying. I was baffled by his wheezy growl of words. The English I was learning at school was nothing like this. We were taught to open our mouths and make round clear sounds. Every word was a flower opening out in my mouth, I imagined. I had to take care and not crush it. This boy was speaking through clenched teeth. The words, it seemed to me, edged themselves out of the corner of his mouth all squished up and senseless. When I didn't budge or say anything he sidled up to me and said with alarm, 'Ye're no very gabby, pal. D'ye no like foo'ball?'

Like somebody winding up a clock, a grasshopper whirred in the spiny weeds behind us. It was time I said something to this boy who was eyeing me with a puzzled look.

'I'm bad at English.' I shrugged and kicked the gravel at my feet apologetically.

'D'ye no ken English? Ye're no kiddin' me oan.' He thrust his pinched face up close to mine and looked curiously at me. 'Ye wouldnae be dotty, would ya?' he said and then glanced around him warily. A wind stirred the whins and tossed their small cups of fragrant yellow. I took a long sniff of this scented air and spoke slowly, belabouring every word.

'My name is Charlie Sharkey and I like football.'

He pondered this, grinned and then reached out his hand, assertively.

'Gi' us yer haun. We're pals. Ah'm nae better, I canny speak the Gaelic.'

He drags me out onto the field with a playful tug, grabs the ball, throws it high in the air and calls, 'C'moan; gi' it the header noo.' As it dropped, I launched myself at it and, with a bold nudge of the head, sent it spinning into the goal mouth.

'Bliddy good header,' he shouted, giving me an approving nod. We played in silence. Jimmy, with his wily moves, easily got the better of me in close tackles, but I could outrun him when I managed to duck his challenge.

'There's nothin' like foo'ball,' he declared when we sat down for a breather. 'It wouldnae be the same wi'oot it. I want to play for Celtic when I'm a big yin,' he beamed at me, all fired up with excitement. Globs of sweat twinkled on his thin cheeks and on the jaggedy bristles of his cropped hair. Close by, at a small quarry by the lake, I could see a neighbour sifting gravel through a coarse riddle. That was how Jimmy spoke; the words spluttered from his mouth with a gravelly whoosh.

Now I was making out a word here and there, enough to get the gist of what he said, but I wished I could really talk to him, tell him things about myself. I lay back and imagined a future where I could speak English fluently. Above us, the sky was a grown-up face, lathered with big soapy clouds. Suddenly the sun cut through and gleamed like a new razor blade. A smooth face of blue looked down at us.

'It's hot the noo,' he said, picking up the ball. 'I'm off doon the way. Ma granny is makin' dinner and I'll hivtae hurry.'

To our right a patch of water lilies brightened up the lake. It looked to me like a table laid out with dark green plates and glossy white cups. I wanted to say this to Jimmy, but I didn't have the confidence to express it.

'Ye hivtae come up to our hoose if ye got the time. I'm holidaying wi' ma granny,' he said, and slouched off across the bog.

I had started learning English in the primary school, but the summer I met Jimmy I got a chance to put it into practice. At first I spoke slowly, testing each word as if it were a dodgy stepping stone across a swamp. I'd brace myself for these crossings. To get from the beginning to the end of a sentence without slipping into the morass was an achievement. I must have sounded idiotic to him when I stumbled on a word and fell into incoherence. He would look at me bemused and say, 'Ye hivtae speed it up, pal. Naebody speaks like tha' if yer nae saft in the head.' His taunting made me more determined than ever to learn. For a while it was just anxious bluster and a clumsy persistence that kept me going, but then I began to pick it up and even speak it with a noticeable Glasgow accent. It was exiting to dash off a sentence without making a muddle of it and when I began to understand and respond easily to his screechy cackle, I was elated.

The capital of my child's world was Glasgow, more real to me then than Dublin, our own capital. The continuous to-ing and fro-ing of people between our place and Glasgow familiarised me with that city; its grimy streets and its smelly tenements. My father gave me *No Mean City* to read, a raw, gritty novel about the squalid grimness and brutal violence of the Glasgow slums. This angry, bitter, rasping testimony of working-class life in the

Gorbals, an area well known to my parents, did not diminish my enthusiasm for the city. Its nitty-gritty bleakness made Glasgow stir in my blood like a heartbeat.

My mother and father met in Glasgow in the late 1940s. Auntie Biddy, a widow, had a house in Ballater Street close to the Gorbals and her two younger sisters, Mary and Agnes, lodged with her whenever they were working in Glasgow. Mary was the one that my father fancied. He met her at some Irish get-together in Crown Street. At the time, he was working on a farm in Ayrshire but that weekend he came up to Glasgow for a wee break. He and Mary, a slim, attractive, feisty girl-about-town, became friends but, much to his dismay, she showed no romantic interest whatsoever in him. Instead, she foisted this tall, gauche, plain-looking man on Agnes, her pretty but simple-minded younger sister. Agnes, having no education or particular skills, worked in low, mean servile jobs – be it as a tatie-hoker on the farms or as a herring girl gutting fish in the Shetlands. When my father met her she was working as a skivvy in a big house in Pollokshaws. I think he liked the wild, untamed streak of unknowingness in her which made her a challenging prospect. He himself was quietly diffident, calm and patient and maybe needed the maverick in her to give a bit of edge to his equanimity. He proposed to her on Glasgow Green one Saturday evening after a long stroll along Argyle Street and Sauchiehall Street. She accepted without hesitation, glad to get an upstanding, solid man who would care for her.

Meeting Jimmy made Glasgow even more immediate to me. His urban world of department stores, tenements, Celtic football matches, *Oor Willie and the Broons*, cowboy films, gang fights, the *Dandy* and the *Beano* and pop music fascinated me. He was equally intrigued, I think, by the world I lived in; my wild mountain playground, my cows and sheep and hens, my scampering nimbleness up hills, over ditches, across bogs. I showed him life on a farm: a cow being bulled; how to harness a donkey, bottle-feed a calf, foot turf, handle frogspawn.

That summer I became conscious for the first time of the difference between Gaelic and English. It was liberating becoming aware of the two languages, two different ciphers to denote the same thing. How could '*cnoc*' be 'hill'? I favoured '*cnoc*' because it sounded more rounded to me. It seemed to fit those bulbously plump swells that surrounded me. 'Hill' seemed to be too slender, too blunt. It sounded more like an upthrust, a stone pillar. I began to see that each word in Irish, each word in English had its own precise shape, its own particular soundscape. You couldn't take a word from one language and have it reproduced exactly in the other language. It wasn't possible to have a perfect likeness. You could find a counterpart, of course, but it was never the exact same.

'*Fuinneog*' for all practical purposes was the equivalent of 'window' but there was a huge difference in how they looked, how they behaved in the sound structure of a sentence. The common greeting '*Dia dhuit*' was theologically loaded compared to 'hello', its more laid-back, secular counterpart in English. 'Fridge' was called '*cuisneoir*' in Irish. We didn't have a fridge at home, but I knew what it was from a shop in Gortahork. It was where they kept ice cream. Fridge was an ice-cold box that shut tight with a rubbery, sludgy snap. '*Cuisneoir*' I'd never heard as a spoken word, a living word in the mouth of any local. When I asked somebody about it, they said '*Ó sin Gaeilge mhaide na leabhar*' – 'that's the wooden Irish of the books'. It was a school word and, because of my distaste for school, a dead word. Now

I know it's an apt evocation of the fridge in Gaeilge. It comes from '*cuisne*', meaning frosty or cold haze. It's the kind of linguistic adaptability I admire. Using a root word in Gaelic and extending and enlarging its meaning, its '*brí*'. '*Brí*' in Irish signifies 'meaning' but also means strength and vigour. In short, having two languages enabled me to view the world through two different lenses. I was beginning to see that each lens was tilted differently.

Mid-morning, Jimmy came for me. I heard his jerky, tuneless whistle as he approached the house and then the quick tap and patter of his football as he bounced it up and down on our flagged doorstep. It was his way to alert me that he was there.

'What are ye daein'?' he said, when I came to the door.

'I'll have to take the cows up to the bog for a bit of grazing.'

'OK, amigo, let's mosey along.' He liked to play cowboys when we were out herding the cattle.

The air was moist and heavy with the buttery scent of gorse as we drove the cows up the gravelly road by the Dúloch. We sauntered behind them, listening to the easy wheeze of their breathing and the swish of their tails swatting horseflies. The low-slung hammock of their bellies swayed gently as they trogged along, swerving their heads to lop off the tall spindly grass that grew by the wayside. Mrs Kennedy in her cream-coloured Hudson chugged past, leaving a fine drape of yellow dust hanging around us. We could still hear the clomp and rattle of her vehicle as she bumped along the narrow rutty track beyond Loch an Ghainimh. Jimmy plucked a blossom from a fuchsia bush that grew by the road and twirled it in his fingers. I remarked that it was like a dancing girl in a red costume.

'Oh aye,' he said, and poked a finger inside to reveal a purple petticoat.

'I wannae take off her knickers.' He seemed tense and excitable as he pulled at the purple petals.

'Ah wish tae God I had a girl,' he said, and there was a strange yearning in his voice. I sensed a need in him and although I wasn't sure what it was, it unsettled me.

'You're too young,' I said, somewhat abruptly. I was trying to make little of what he said.

'Ye're kiddin' me oan. I'm nearly thirteen and rarin' tae go.' He puffed out his chest in a show of manliness and groped his crotch.

'Ah'm no jokin', pal. I wannae dae it.'

I felt a little awkward and walked ahead saying nothing. It was like seeing somebody with their trousers down.

On the rise above the Dúloch we could see Errigal, Achla and Muckish, a long, high line of blue-black mountains against a misty sky. They were the Black Hills of Dakota, Jimmy said. I was more inclined to see them as Mexican bandits, each wearing a big moustache of scree and a jaunty sombrero of mist.

'Hi ho Silver away!' Jimmy hollered as he crouched low on his imaginary steed and galloped around the cows. We were trail hands, he explained, out on the open range, rounding up and branding long-horn steers.

'Och, come on coos, gi' us a bit of a run.' He wanted a stampede, a braying headlong lunge up the road, but however much we prodded them the cows wouldn't oblige. They just lumbered along with unflappable heaviness and ignored us. They knew exactly where they were going and when we passed the fork in the road at Loch an Ghainimh they veered right and down a stony path to graze the dewy grass at the head of the lake. After a while they sloshed through the water and headed up to Páirc Mhéabha, a small green pasture that lay like a bottle-green island in a speckled sea of heather. They would graze the sedgy grass until evening time and then drift back home by themselves.

A high, bulky turf stack stood on a bit of hard ground above the lake. This was Tombstone, Jimmy said, and we were gunslingers on a fierce shoot-out in the town. Our guns were forked pine sticks which we picked up in the bog. We chased each other around the turf stack, guns blazing. Bang! Bang! Bang! A hail of bullets whizzed from our mouths. Suddenly Jimmy noticed something. A single file of sheep looming on the crest of a nearby hill were mounted Sioux warriors ready to sweep down and attack us. We could hear their bleating war cries.

'So whit are we supposed to dae?' he said, scanning the horizon with a quick, cautious look.

'We'll ride away on our horses,' I suggested feebly.

'Oh aye, we'll gi' it a try.'

With that, he jumped on my back and whacked me on the rump with the palm of his hand. 'Hi ho Silver away,' he said, spurring me on. I snorted, tossed my head wildly and broke into a lolloping gallop. The suck and plash of my boots across soggy bog sounded faintly like the clatter of hooves.

'We have tae hotfoot it out of here, Silver, before them Injuns come doon and catch us.'

I tried to make a dash but stumbled and fell in a patch of spongy moss, Jimmy on top of me. The moss was as soft as the squashy mass of straw and feathers that my mother stuffed into our tick once a year. I felt Jimmy's hot breath stirring the downy hair at the back of my neck and the press of his body hard against mine pinned me to the ground. I slithered out from beneath him and lay face up in the moss. He lay crouched up against me, his face close to mine. He rucked up his forehead and peered at me with a strained expression. I knew that he was anxious.

'Would ye like a wee geek at my willie?' he said, hoarsely. Before I could reply he zipped open his fly and took out a small, girthy member. It was pumped up and solid as a bicycle tyre. I blushed and looked away. Grey tree stumps jutted out of the bog, all wizened and twisted. Like old crones they sat there and stared.

'Naebody is near us, pal,' Jimmy said, pleadingly. A snipe, like a kid goat bleating, cried at the water's edge. I glimpsed at Jimmy and saw that he had shut his eyes. He was fondling himself with the tips of his fingers. His brown puckered sac, ringed by a frizzle of red hair, lay snug between his legs like a nest hidden in scrabby bog grass.

Showing me his privates in such a bold, unashamed way made me uneasy and yet I was gripped by what he was doing. I felt a sharp stir in my own groin area, an urgent stiffening that confused me. I didn't know whether I was going to soar up into the sky or burst out in a blaze of fire. Maybe my body had split open, I thought, in a sort of ripening. It had something to do with growing up and with sex. In the schoolyard the older boys talked about sex as if it were a hunger, an ache. I had often watched a cow being bulled, so I had some notion of what they meant. When a cow was in heat she became bothered and frisky and slimed at the mouth. She had to be serviced before she calmed down again. Many times I saw these hectic couplings when I dragged one or other of our own cows on a rope to be serviced by a local bull. The bull would snort and paw the ground, then nose her hindquarters with fussy care before straddling her flanks and slamming into her. When the business was over the cow seemed relieved and always trotted back home without any bother.

'Pit yer haun oan it,' Jimmy urged. His words were slurred and he sounded desperate. A milky white mist was closing in over the bog like a bed covering.

'Come oan, please.' He grimaced as if a twinge of pain shot through him. I gripped his pink bulge the way my mother held a cow's teat and stroked it gently, setting up the steady rhythm of milking.

'Hold hahd,' he said, writhing under me as if a terrible helplessness came over him.

'Are you alright?' I said, thinking he was in distress.

'Oh aye-aye-aye,' he croaked and a gob of white ooze like wet bog cotton pumped out of him and splattered across the moss. I had no notion what this gluey spew was and I felt frightened in case I had crushed something soft and frail inside him. But whatever happened he seemed to have got a charge out of it. He sat there with a big grin on his face and wiped away the seep with a hanky.

'This is great, intit? Oh aye, cowboy, this is the life, eh.'

There was nothing I could say so I just nodded. Maybe this was something cowboys did after a gunfight. Actually, the sharp brassy odour that I was getting off his willie was like the smell of a shot cartridge. My neighbour had a shotgun and I knew that acrid smell. Jimmy zipped up his trousers and stood looking out at a grey stretch of rippling lake. He was silent except for the suck of his breath. Small modest waves lisped at the shore. I wanted to say something about what had happened, but there was a silence around my words. I knew that our wet hot moment on the cushiony bed of moss had in it strange stirrings of the flesh and a sensing of the future. I had stumbled upon a new knowledge that was both a strength and a threat, a power and a sorrow. When I tried to speak I felt a nervous twitch at the corner of my mouth. My words fizzled out like the white spasm of waves that broke softly below me.

Jimmy turned around and gave me a poke in the ribs.

'We have tae go doon to the gulch and round up the mavericks.' With that he gave a swift welt of the hand to his behind and galloped down the turf bank to where the cows grazed in a grassy hollow. I followed behind, grave and silent. A startled grouse rose out of the heather a little to my left and flapped across the water, its husky cackle so much like Jimmy's clenched speech. I picked a little blossom of purple heather and twirled it between my fingers. I wished that I could find a word as weightless as that flower to describe what had happened.

That Sunday we were the first out of the church after Mass was over and were waiting by the gate for Jimmy's granny, who lingered behind to light up some candles, when he nudged me in the arm.

'There's Johnny. He's a Teddy boy.'

There was a wariness in his voice that made me take notice. I followed his gaze and saw in that dull, colourless heave of people swelling out of the church a tall, wiry young man wearing the most dazzling rigout I had ever seen. He swung down the steps with a slow, brash swagger. Some people gaped at him with curiosity, others gave him disapproving looks. He eyed them all with a sneer. It went well, I thought, with the strut and the flashy dash of his dress; a blue, long-draped jacket with shimmery black velvet lapels, black tapered trousers so tight they clung teasingly to his legs, a cherry-red shirt with a dangling strip of green tie and blue shoes, soft and pointed at the toes. He was the showiest man I had ever seen on a Sunday morning in Gortahork, and he was a Teddy boy.

Teddy boys had a bad name. I knew that because I'd heard them called thugs and hooligans and prigs. Glasgow was full of them, my father told me. One evening on Sauchiehall Street he saw a Teddy boy flick a knife and slash another man's face. In my mind they were a rowdy, brawling, scruffy, good-for-nothing lot. Nobody mentioned that they were snappy dressers.

Now I was seeing for the first time what a Teddy boy really looked like and I was impressed. Granted, Johnny had a menacing air about him. He was sullen and defiant, wildly savage, maybe. Even murderous for all I knew, but I didn't care; I just loved his sharp dressy flamboyance and the sassy insolence with which he carried it off.

At the gate he swung around to Jimmy.

'Holidaying, eh?'

I saw Jimmy gulp and swallow as if caught off guard.

'Aye. I'm wi' ma granny up the road.'

I couldn't keep my eyes off the carefully styled black glitter of his hair. Quaffed up boldly at the front with a duck's-arse crease at the back, it shone with a greased shininess as if polished. I was thinking how long it took him to shape it when someone shouted from beyond the gate.

'Ye're nae bliddy good, Johnny.'

I saw his face harden. He turned around, a glare of hostility in his eyes, and moved towards two lumpy young men with dark, spotty faces who stood facing him outside the gate. They had nothing of the snazzy appeal of Johnny. Compared to him, they looked old-fashioned and dowdy in their wrinkled, mousy-grey suits. From their speech I knew they were Scotties but I couldn't pick up much of what they said. Words crept out of their mouths; they were all hunched up and tough like the local hard men who slipped out of church before the Mass was over. All I heard was a gabble of menacing sounds. When I asked Jimmy what they were arguing about, he replied in a hushed voice, 'Johnny is going out wi' their sister and they dinnae like it.'

Suddenly, the smaller of the two, a mean-looking fellow with thin coppery hair and a slash across his cheek like the slit in a money box, charged head down into Johnny and tried to knock him off balance. He was too deft for that. A split second before he bullocked into him, Johnny quickly sidestepped, but not before he clouted his assailant with a whacking punch to the face.

The man stumbled but managed to steady himself against a parked car. He stood there grimacing with pain, his hand held to his face, a trickle of blood dripping off his fingers.

The other man kept jerking his right shoulder up and down in a nervous twitch and looked panicky. I think he'd have made a run for it if he hadn't been afraid of losing face. When Johnny challenged him he made a swipe at him with his fist, but it was a wild swing, a wheeling flab of a thing that failed to connect. They grappled, pushing back and forth, but he was no match for Johnny who clawed at his windpipe and left him gasping. When Johnny pinned him up against the wall, his face had the same blotched yellow colour as the wild mushrooms growing at his feet. Johnny released his grip when the man's eyes began to roll in his head.

'What's the score wi' ye now?' Johnny growled into his face. The man sucked for air, then expelled it in a whooshing sound like a plug being pulled in a washbasin full of water. He tried to say something but no words came, only a hollow, gurgling sound. Johnny, his face red with rage, jutted out his strong jaw and goaded him on gleefully: 'Come oot wi' it before I fall doon laughin'.'

'You fuckin' wait, Johnny,' he croaked out at last, puffing with the effort to speak.

By now a ring of eagerly peering faces had closed in on the action. Remarks were quietly exchanged back and forth among the crowd.

'By cripes that dandy fella can handle himself.'

'You wouldn't think that with the fancy cut of him.'

'Them Scotties are wicked for fightin'.'

'Aye boy, and it's worse they're gettin'.'

'Look at them two slobs, there's no fight left in them.'

Bruised and dazed, Johnny's two opponents crouched by the

wall and whinged among themselves. They had the slinky look
of beaten dogs. The smaller one held a hanky to his bleeding nose
and kept sniffling. The other one had a noticeable red weal
notched across his Adam's apple and it gave his pale, drained face
a little colour. As a show of defiance, the smaller one shook a
bloody hanky at Johnny.

'It's no' over. We'll dae ye in, John.'

'Dae what?' Johnny sneered. He lit a cigarette, took a hard drag
at it, and flipped the lit match in their faces. 'Ye're nae match for
me, boys.'

The taller one opened his mouth to say something but could
only manage a thin squeal like a whimpering dog. He clutched
his throat in desperation and held it until he got his voice back.

'Ye fuckin' wait, Johnny.' And he snapped his jaw shut as if
gagged by rage. He gave Johnny a black look and then he and his
fat butty crossed the road and hobbled down the footpath towards
Gallaghers' shop.

'What d'ya think?' Johnny grunted as he strode past Jimmy, a
look of bemusement on his surly face.

'I don't know how ye dae it, Johnny,' Jimmy blurted out as if
what he had seen was scarcely credible. Johnny walked away, head
held high.

As he crossed the road he kept blowing smoke rings. It looked
as if he were flipping coins in the air like a magician and making
them disappear. He was gorgeous, I thought, a star of glitz and
style, my man of the hour. I knew I could worship him and it
would be more meaningful than anything I experienced in
church that morning.

Because my handwriting was unusually scrawly I often used
large block letters to make myself clear, especially if I was writing
a letter. It occurred to me as I watched Johnny walk away, bold
as brass in his glamour, that he was using clothes to make a block-

letter statement about himself. My reading of it was that clothes, stance and pose were, for him, a way of highlighting his character, showing us his spirit. I hadn't thought much about clothes until then, certainly not clothes as a way to assert identity. I looked at myself and felt embarrassed by my shabby appearance.

Johnny was gone but he left in me a yearning for what was daring, for what was risky; an ache that throbbed like a thorn in my flesh.

Dark brooding clouds were sweeping across the sky. Rain was on the way but in the meantime patches of sun like a white gauzy plaster soothed the potholes on the road and the cracks along the footpath.

One evening later that week I was out for a stroll to pass the time and I chanced upon Johnny at Loch na Stacán, a small reed lake in a bog of old tree stumps, a short walk from my house.

It was a still, balmy evening and as I dandered along the road I could hear sheep cropping grass in a rough field to my left. A blackbird sang in the wild hedging by the wayside, and, when I tried to whistle its tune, it flitted off, annoyed, leaving a little bough twitching like someone pointing an angry finger in my face. On the rise about Niall Rua's house, pausing to watch a rabbit hop and bob through humps of heather, I was drawn unexpectedly to singing down by the lake. Strange, I thought to myself, locals didn't meet down there and they never sang *that* sort of song. Curious to see who it was, I sneaked across the ridge, keeping myself out of sight in the tall grass.

Out of his snazzy Sunday wear, I didn't recognise him at first in a white T-shirt and jeans. It was the oily gleam in his hair that gave him away. He was dancing at the water's edge with a dark-haired girl in a tight red dress with black spots, which made her look like a ladybird. They danced a giddy, quickstepping shuffle and while they danced they sang the kind of songs that made me want to stomp about and shake whenever I heard them on the radio. I was just becoming aware of music that thumped in your head, pulsed through your body and made your heart pound like a Red Indian drum. When it came on the radio something inside me wanted to wiggle out and go wild. I loved the sweet choking agony of 'Wake Up

Little Susie' and the reckless driving rhythms of 'Johnny B. Goode'.

Johnny was now strumming an imaginary guitar and, in sweet unison, they sang 'Rave On', another song I knew from the radio. Then he grabbed her by the waist, there was a kissing tussle and the two of them collapsed in the grass in fits of laughter. I sensed that they didn't want anybody to see them so I dragged myself along the ground and lay low in a covering of tall green ferns where I could watch them without being seen.

She leaned back, arched her body a little and in one quick slither eased her panties down her legs and tossed them at Johnny.

'C'moan,' she pleaded hoarsely. He stood up, undid his jeans and let them flap loosely around his feet. His cock stood up, fat and stout, in a bushy patch of black. It was thick like the neck of a goose. A terrible urge came over me to fondle it. It would take all of my two small hands to encircle its beefy girth, but that made it all the more exciting. I trembled all over thinking about the curious happiness it would give me to squeeze it. I wanted to rush down and throw myself at it, sniff it, tickle it, nibble it. My body was straining at the leash, raring to go, but something kept me from breaking cover – a knowingness, perhaps, that her sulky red lips and her leggy openness were more to his taste than anything I could give him. It was Johnny who excited me and not her. I wondered at that, but was too gripped by the moment's pleasure to bother myself about it. A faint breeze, like a finger stroking the reeds, made them sigh.

'How come ye're no wearin' a Frenchie?' she asked him and sounded cross.

'Could nae get any in the shop in Gortahork. Sold oot,' Johnny said and he laughed.

'Oh aye, very funny. Ye kin just wait 'til ye get protection. I'm nae getting pregnant in the bogs of Donegal.'

'I'm havin' ye oan, Sally. I always carry me wellies in case I hav tae do a bit of sloggin' in the bog. Look in my pocket there.'

She took something out of the blue denim jacket that she was using as a headrest and handed it to him. It was a clear glossy sleeve and when he slipped it over his hardened cock it looked wet and slushy in the evening sunshine. This was, I guessed, a French letter, and although I had heard about them I had never seen one. Until I met Jimmy the month before, I had some vague notion that it prevented a woman from having a baby, but how was still a mystery to me. After our odd carry-on in the bog when Jimmy's penis spewed white, I had mulled it over in my mind and realised that this milky release was what came when people were having sex. Up to then I wasn't sure what the older boys at school meant when they boasted about 'tossing off' and 'shooting their load'. I had no idea that any fluid other than urine could issue from my penis. Until this discovery I had a notion that a man had to piss into a woman before she could have a baby. It was evident to me now that it was this seedy fluid and not urine that made babies. Thinking about this made my own penis swell and jerk, and when I rubbed it I experienced for myself the hot, tickly spill of sex. I realised that it was this powerful spurt of pleasure, which made my body shudder and my breath come in short rapid gasps, that Jimmy and the boys at school craved so much. I was astonished that when this groping root in my groin moved, it made me heedless to everything else. It was an urge stronger and needier than hunger and I knew that it would never go away. Like an appetite, the hungering ache for this pleasure would always be with me.

I knew exactly why Johnny had to have this wrapper around his penis, especially now that he was on top of her. Pincer-like, she had her legs hooked across his back and when she heaved underneath him she was a swirl of black dots tightening around him. He was in the clutches of a huge, needy ladybird.

'Johnny! Johnny!' she cried out, and when her calls gave way to low, coarse grunts he got frantic and slapped against her, vigorous as a bull. Then it was all over and they lay slumped against each other as if winded. That's how I felt when I touched myself. Sex was both a wild stirring and a soothing that left the body sleepy yet strangely awake.

The blue light of evening was giving way to a faint coppery dark. A heady smell of heather swept across the bog. Johnny threw back his head and sniffed the air.

'My ma says when she's going oot to the lavvy that she's going to the bog. I think she always carries this fresh smell in her head.'

'It's better than the lavvy smells in oor close too,' she said, pulling up her panties. She stood, brushed specks of heather off her dress and tidied her hair.

'Would you live here, Sally?' Johnny asked her as he buttoned up his jeans.

'It's alright for a holiday, but it's nae good for a life,' she said and mopped her face with a hanky. 'It's too lonely, Johnny.'

'You wouldnae be lonely with me, Sally.'

'It's no' you, Johnny. It's the bogs. They're haunted. I wouldnae get a wink of sleep here.'

'No, I'd be humpin' ye all night, Sally.'

'O aye, great balls of fire,' she said and playfully grabbed his crotch. 'Too much love drives a man insane.'

'Good Golly Miss Molly,' Johnny sang out in a high-pitched voice and feigned an injury to his groin. He then dropped a small stone into the French letter and flung it away out into the reeds. They watched it plop into the water and make little wavy rings to the shore.

'Some lucky trout'll hav a sleepin' bag tonight,' Johnny said.

'Let's go on doon to the pub, Johnny, before the ghosts come oot of these bogs.'

Arm in arm they walked across to a whinbush where they had hidden their bicycles. I didn't leave my hiding place until I could no longer hear the whirr and click of their wheels. Then it was safe to come out. I could still see the press of their bodies in the flattened grass. I lay down on my back where they were and imagined that I was with Johnny, belly to belly, thigh to thigh, my hands on the white, creamy bump of his buttocks.

The Cuban Missile Crisis in 1962 was an event that filled me with dread. Everyone was talking about 'an atomic war' and how we would have to stay indoors until it was over and cover up our windows and seal our doors. Big dust clouds would block off the sun and all that was green on earth would wither and die. It would be winter forever. I wondered how we were going to survive a long spell in a shut-up house without sufficient food. We would soon run out of the little we had and then we would, more than likely, starve to death. Just as well, because the world after 'the atomic war' would be a savage place to live in. For a few days, I lived in fear and kept a close watch on the sky for any sign of a mushrooming cloud.

My father assured me that the Russians would back down and that Kennedy would have his way but nonetheless it was all the talk among the neighbours one evening in late October 1962.

'It'll be some rammy, I'm tellin' ye. Them Russians won't be easy to beat. Sure they have the big bomb themselves.'

'Will you wheesht, man. Kennedy'll flatten them before they have a chance to press the button.'

'That Kennedy fella hasn't a splink of sense, if you ask me. He's as hot-headed as bedamnt, putting the world in jeopardy like this.'

'Will ye steady up, man. He has no choice. He has to stand up to them bliddy Commies or let them take over the world.'

'It's a sad day, I'm tellin' ye. One of them atomic bombs going off in London will finish the whole damn lot of us here too. There's no place safe any more.'

That evening our wee glen looked so homely in the cosy light of the setting sun. Every hill, field and house glowed with a settled contentment. I wondered was this going to be the last rosy sunset I was going to see on the earth. It was a troubling thought and I felt tearfully sad. Two frisky heifers jostled with each other over a low dry-stone wall below where I sat. One was sleek and black with a white spot on its forehead; the other was bony and reddish brown, a runt of an animal. I likened the black one to Kennedy from the photo I had seen of him in the *Irish Press*: a black-suited, handsome man, tall and trim with a firm, manly smile. I was glad when blackie dunted the runt and she took off down the fields, as if in a huff, lashing her tail and braying loudly.

Nora John's puppy-dog, who was chasing an old tawny cat, whirled about when it saw me and, with a lot of tail-wagging, clambered up into my lap and polished my face with wet licks. As I held him, puppy-soft against me, I prayed that this lovely world would be spared. The next day we heard on the radio that the Russians had backed off. Kennedy was a hero and, even better still, he was one of our own.

My father was very interested in current affairs and when Dan and Mylie, two bachelor brothers, bought a television – the first in our neighbourhood – we often went there at night to watch the news and programmes like *That Was the Week that Was*, *Dr Finlay's Casebook* and Cassius Clay fights. Vietnam was always in the headlines; a village going up in a big burst of flames, screaming children, muddy-faced American soldiers patrolling the jungles.

The same recurring images of faraway death and destruction bored me until I saw a boy who had lost his leg in the bombing stare out at me, his face contorted with pain. That sad, pitiful look gave Vietnam a human face. It was no longer a distant occurrence. Because it was happening to *that* boy, it became horrendously immediate to me. I couldn't watch the reports without thinking about him, wondering how he was and hoping to get a second glimpse of him. For about a month or two, the boy from Vietnam I would never meet became a real presence in my life. I wanted to be by his side and help him to hobble along on his one good leg. I would be his support and playmate. We would be blood brothers, living for each other.

The outside world, whether I liked it or not, was seeping into my consciousness.

Part Three

Other days we went for long walks around the table . . .

Roger McGough

After I finished primary school, I wasn't too keen on any further schooling, but when a boy from my class that I was fond of enrolled at the local tech, I decided to follow him. I was encouraged by the fact that if I didn't like it I could pack up and leave at any time.

If the first day at primary school was misery, the first day at the tech was magical. It changed my life forever.

In the afternoon, a tall, youngish, fair-haired teacher strolled into our classroom, looked us over calmly, and smiled. His name was Mr Lally.

'I smell fear in this room,' he began, 'it's the kind of fusty smell you get in rooms that have been closed up for a long time.'

He paced in front of the class, sniffing the air inquisitively.

'I'm getting it here and here.' He leaned forward slightly and beamed a big smile at us.

'You are the rooms that reek of fear,' he confided in a hushed tone. 'We need a good gust of laughter to freshen up those fearful places.'

Then, without using a word, he acted out a drunk, sloshed out of his mind, cadging on the street until he slumps down and falls into a loud, boozy sleep. He caught the character perfectly; the drunken slouch, the beery hiccups, the straggly walk. It was so funny we roared with laughter. He stood up and gave us an indulgent smile.

'You are not, I hope, laughing at someone who is a down-and-out drunk. That is not a laughing matter. You are laughing at me acting out a drunk.'

I was touched by this subtle difference and the kindness implied by it.

'You cannot learn anything if you are fearful,' he continued. 'We have to trust each other on this journey. Together we are going on an outing in the imagination.'

He picked up a book and read us 'The Road Not Taken' by Robert Frost. His delivery was dramatic, captivating; he held our attention effortlessly. When he finished reading he asked us mischievously, 'What do you think about that poem?'

Jesus, I nearly jumped out of my skin with surprise. I'd never been asked that kind of question at primary school, where there was no discussion, where we were empty vessels waiting to be filled to the brim with facts. This was exhilaratingly new. Smiling, he waited for a response. After a long, awkward pause, I cleared my throat and ventured an opinion.

'Sir, the poet is saying that the wee lane is far better to walk on than the big road.'

'What is your name?' he asked eagerly.

'Charlie Sharkey.'

'Well, Charlie, I want to hear what you think. Is the less-travelled path more tempting to you than the main road?'

'Yes, sir.'

'Why?'

That question fazed me a little, until I thought of something my father had said to me the day we came across clusters of the sweetest blackberries I had ever tasted in a grassy lane beyond our house.

'Because you'll always find the best blackberries down the back lanes,' I replied after a pause.

He gave me a steadfast, reassuring look.

'Thank you, Charlie. That's a very convincing reason for walking the byroads, especially now that it's September, blackberry-picking time. Would anyone else like to comment?' he continued, regarding us with an inviting grin.

By now everybody was itching to say something, kids who had a dull, throttled look coming into the class were now fired up and swinging their arms vigorously to get the teacher's attention. With a bold snap of the fingers or a firm 'Silence, please', he kept the lively hubbub of our enthusiasm in check so that everyone had a chance to have their say.

Whatever you said was received graciously, weighed and pondered by our smiling teacher. I liked how he used the poem as a prompt to get us talking. Did we really have a choice in life, he queried, or were we, by and large, predisposed to behave in a certain way? Was it fate or free will that determined the course of our actions? I thrived under this sort of tuition. Class was no longer a dreaded chore but a welcome challenge. I no longer sat numbly in my seat, filled with fear. I clamoured to be heard. He had a rare knack of getting us all to express ourselves. Even the two or three who still squirmed with shyness in their self-protective shells were beginning to make a breakthrough. A spark of laughter, a squeak, a wee push of confidence, and soon he would have them out of their timidity and voicing their opinions. We respected him, partly because he listened, really listened, to what you had to say, and partly because of his fulsome praise even if you only attempted a hesitant word.

But above and beyond all of that was his presence – his sparkling eyes, his boundless energy, his whole-hearted attentiveness to what he was doing – that beguiled us that very first day and delightfully eased us out of ourselves.

'Remember the drunk I acted out for you at the beginning of the class?' he continued. 'Are some people programmed to become boozers, for instance?' he asked. 'Are some others, like Robert Frost, who wrote this poem, destined to become poets?'

A spotty boy with a thick, lazy voice, who was mostly quiet up to then, spoke up.

'There's a fella beside me at home, sir, and he's always on the tear. I heard them say there's drink in his blood.'

'What do you think that means?' the teacher asked.

'Sure, that's aisy, sir. There's a brave drouth on him.'

'A steady drinker, is he?'

'Naw, sir. He has a wild dose of the shakes when he's fluthered.'

We howled at that, and so did the teacher.

'I walked myself right into that, didn't I?' he admitted readily when he got his breath back from laughing. 'Give Johnny a big hand for his efforts to keep up our spirits.'

He talked to us about language and how it's taken for granted, just like breathing.

'It's the sixth element,' he said, 'as vital to us as air and water, earth, sky and fire.'

Language was, in fact, he pointed out, closely allied to the elements: like air, we thrived on it daily to get by; like water, it took us on voyages whenever we read a novel or a poem. When we were angry it had fire in it, when we were rude it was often earthy; when we prayed it had sky in it and rose up into the wide blue yonder.

'We speak as effortlessly as we breathe, and rarely do we take stock of either of these two functions,' he claimed.

He asked us to sit up, shut our eyes and breathe deeply, focusing all the time on the flow, the in and out of air. None of us had ever experienced breathing in this way before, and at first we giggled awkwardly, but he coaxed us into it with level-headed calmness. I began in a wheezy huff and puff, but as I became absorbed in the exercise my breathing gave way to a pleasurable hum like the purring of a contented cat or a breeze in a dreepy hedge. Becoming attentive to the rhythm of my own breathing relaxed me. The commotion in my head quietened down. I noticed myself becoming still, almost sleepy, soothed on the flow of breath. And yet I was perfectly alert, so much so that I could hear the boy next to me flutter his eyelashes.

'That is what I call a breathtaking experience,' he announced with a big grin at the end of our exercise. By now I was heady with happiness and wishing that this astonishing class would go on and on forever.

A poem is also a breathing body of words, he told us, but you have to read it aloud to hear the gulp and gasp of it. I understood that. The poem came alive when you read it out loud. My father's fireside recitations taught me that. Whenever I read a poem at home I spoke it out so that I could hear it take to the air. It seemed to skim and dip and soar as it rose off my tongue. It was like setting free a bird. The teacher was now asking would any of us like to come up and read 'The Road Not Taken' in front of the class. I was quick off the mark, and before any of the other boys could say 'boo' I was out of my seat and offering to read.

'Splendid,' he shouted, patting me on the back with generous enthusiasm when I finished. 'Robert Frost himself, I'm sure, would be pleased with that rendition. You made his poem breathe beautifully.'

For the first time ever I had been praised at school and made to feel special. It was a lovely moment of joy, and I let it seep into me like a sudden burst of warm sunshine. The boys applauded and then class was over. At the door, as he was going out, he turned around to us and sniffed the air.

'Fresh confidence! Yes, that's what I'm smelling. Keep oozing it out, boys. And remember,' and he grinned widely at me, 'the untrodden path is where the best blackberries grow.'

'Jesus, I didn't have a bloody notion what he was at, but it was some crack, wasn't it?' a tall boy with bright, buttony eyes that looked as if they were sewn onto his face roared at us when he had gone.

School could be fun after all, I thought to myself. For a start, I had found a teacher who inspired me. That was promising.

You went to the tech to pick up a trade. Unsurprisingly, the curriculum was largely practical and geared towards those who needed a solid grounding in either woodwork or metalwork. Good, useful, workaday training that prepared you for work 'across the water' or, if you were lucky, an apprenticeship at home. Similarly, girls were instructed in domestic and secretarial skills, giving them a good footing so that they could easily step into hotel and office jobs. It was a two-year programme, by which time you passed out of school, hopefully having made the grade and possessing what was called the Group Cert.

Irish, English, Maths, Technical Drawing and Agricultural Science were the other subjects on my course of studies when I signed on at the tech in September 1966. I soon discovered that I had no aptitude whatsoever for woodwork or metalwork. With a saw or a mallet, a file or a drill I was a hazard not only to myself but to everybody around me. In the joinery class, my joints were so out of joint, so shamelessly misshapen, that not even Joseph the saintly carpenter, according to my teacher, could set them right. My classmates pencilled, chiselled and planed with a smooth, fluid rhythm as if it were as easy as ABC. They turned out clean-cut, tight-fitting, shapely work, whereas I, no matter how much I used the spirit level, could neither level out nor straighten up my saggy attempts at joinery. At the workbench I seemed to lose all of my wits and would hardly know how many fingers made five. Our woodwork teacher was a kind, patient, engaging man who did everything at a leisurely pace. He hardly ever raised his voice to scold us, and yet he managed to keep a cheeky bunch of boys within mannerly boundaries. Students respected him, liked his agreeable ways, and did his bidding without any fuss. I remember once handing up a hopelessly ill-fitting dovetail joint for his appraisal. He looked at it closely, trying to find, I think, something positive in it, some reassuring sign of improvement that would be worthy of praise, but no, there was nothing to redeem my wedge-shaped grotesquerie.

'The finesse of joinery, I think, is not for you, Charlie, but, sure, a few nails will always do the job,' he said with a tactful smile, and let me go.

I fared no better at metalwork, and, despite the best efforts of a very brilliant teacher to guide me, I hacked up every scrap of material he gave me into a laughable shapelessness. With wood and metal I was fated to go against the grain, and no helping hand, however solicitous it was, could change my natural clumsiness. My father, who was good with his hands, was always puzzled at my bungling attempts to repair things around the house.

'You're all thumbs, *a chroí*,' he would quip, 'but they'll come in handy when you're out on the road thumbing a lift.'

I had no head for Technical Drawing. I could never square up to those stern, angular demands. I loathed Maths. It was a lingering hostility to the ruthless logic of decimals and fractions that I carried with me from primary school. Agricultural Science was as dry as a burst puffball, and wasn't to my taste at all.

English was the only subject that really got me going, and that was due to Mr Lally and the way he conducted his class with dash and gusto. The oomph with which he said things made the blood pound in my head with excitement. Other classes may have been drearily predictable, but his never failed to surprise. I remember him, for instance, taking a reel-to-reel tape recorder into our class and playing us ocean sounds; the boom of water breaking on rocks, the cry of gulls and a long slush of waves across a pebbly strand. He got us to act out what we heard. Spread out over the classroom, we became a squawking, wing-flapping ocean in motion. He would recite 'Dover Beach', he told us, a poem by Matthew Arnold, but it would be a good idea, he suggested, to let the poem come into the five ports of our senses as if it were the sea. In this way we would become more conscious of the language of the poem, its tumultuous sound waves, its dark depths, its ceaseless dazzle. As he recited I let the poem flow into me. Suddenly I was afloat on a wave of language; in touch with the heave and surge of syllables, the murmurings of vowels, the rumblings of consonants.

In my second year at the tech the Department of Education authorised a new and broader curriculum in vocational schools, which allowed us to stay on for five years and study for the Leaving Cert. The new syllabus retained the practical subjects but introduced a wide range of academic options. Mr Lally, knowing how unhandy I was at woodwork, metalwork and Technical Drawing, got me out of doing these subjects.

It was a relief to be freed from my own fumbling incompetence at the workbench and the drawing board. Instead, I took History and Latin, Geography, Maths, Biology, Irish and English.

It was a fabulous five-year voyage of discovery, with Mr Lally firmly at the helm showing us the way. I remember him telling us about a ship he saw docked in a port and how they were cleaning it up, scraping away the mess of shells that was stuck to the hull before it set out on its next voyage. It occurred to him, he said, that what they were doing was an apt way to approach a poem. We needed, he explained, to sweep away the barnacles, the fixed convictions and the blinkered beliefs that dulled the hull of our wonder, before we voyaged out on the ocean of a poem. If we could get into that unburdened, buoyant state of mind, he claimed, we would meet not only the poem but life itself anew each day. An alert readiness to the text of the poem, to the lessons of life; that, he enthused, was the key to knowledge, the way to wellbeing. The idea of being open to the unexpected, alert and attentive to the immediate, appealed to me.

'A sense of wonder at the world' was how Mr Lally summed up this notion of openness. He would take us sometimes on a walkabout around the grounds of the school, getting us to register in our notebooks one significant detail of what we saw.

'In Irish, the word *file*, poet, means to see. Open up your eyes, boys,' he urged us. 'Be seers.'

I enjoyed noting down these momentary glimpses.

'I couldn't think of anything to see' was how one boy responded to the exercise.

Mr Lally laughed and complimented him on his wordplay.

'Don't think,' he encouraged the boy. 'Just look.'

It certainly made me look at things, see connections, have pithy insights. 'On the tip of a bough, a wee thrush made notes for me.' That's typical of the kind of observation I jotted down while out on these 'Openings' as he called the exercise.

Mr Lally gave us challenging topics to write about, and willed us on to be creative. Once, while studying Emily Dickinson's strange, unsettling poem 'I Felt a Funeral, in My Brain', he brought a small catalogue of surrealist art into the class and introduced us to the eerie, time-warped visions of Dali. He then asked us to imagine that these two were married and living by the sea in Dunfanaghy. 'Miss Dickinson and Mr Dali in Dunfanaghy' was the title he gave us for our homework. It elicited a short poem from me which he praised to the sky.

My husband dozes
Somewhere on the horizon

A surrealist catalogue
Under his head

With a snore
He breaks the duck-egg of dawn

He dreams of a landscape
Of broken watches

A breakfast full
Of time gone nuts

Well for him, no funeral
Passes through his guts.

I was beginning on my journey to words; a journey I had to make on my own, but Mr Lally was preparing me for it, mapping out as best he could the territory through which I was to travel.

One day Mr Lally suggested that I try my hand at writing in Gaelic. I was in fourth year at the time. It never occurred to me to write in my native language. For many it was, of course, an object of ridicule, the oafish tongue of the bogs, a language of backwardness. I must have been picking up on this; getting the impression that Irish was a spent force, belonging to another time, another place, and maybe even believing a little of it.

English was, by far, my preferred mode of writing. At the time I was reading a lot, voyaging by diving into the floodwaters of a book and coming up worlds away. These transports of joy were entirely in English. My three favourite books that year were Mark Twain's *Huckleberry Finn*, Hermann Hesse's *Narzissus and Goldmund* and Jack Kerouac's *On the Road*. On sleepless nights they kept me company and indeed made me, more often than not, a much-contented insomniac. I was so enthralled by English that I hardly gave a thought to Gaelic until that fateful day when Mr Lally asked me to write a poem for a local talent competition. As it happened, I won and that whetted my appetite to explore what kind of poetry was being written in Gaelic. The tech had no library to talk about, only a glass case crammed with a random mix of titles. It did, however, have volumes by the three most noted Irish-language poets of the time.

Seán Ó Ríordáin was the first of these poets to grab my attention. A TB outcast who, during the 1940s, spent long periods in a sanatorium, wrote authentic poems of suffering and self-doubt; poems that grope in the dark, hoping for a foothold on the slippery slopes of uncertainty. And yet, despite the despair so evident in many of them, they are declarations of survival, lighted candles, as it were, in a night of gusting dark. The way that he scrutinises himself, the introspective journeys into his own interior, were so strongly evoked that I felt sometimes as though I was being smothered. Discovering a writer in Gaelic who, like Gerard Manley Hopkins and Emily Dickinson, was engaged in saying the unsayable was a hugely exciting find for me. He was an activator of language, a pusher of it. He made it get up and go. Rather than letting Gaelic speak through him, he forcibly spoke through Gaelic. The given language was often inadequate for his needs. The risky business of self-scrutiny forced him to shape a language all of his own. It was stimulating to read him from that point of view, to encounter an exciting, individualist expressiveness which was so utterly new to me in Gaelic. As a teenager, starting off on the quest for my unknown self, these poems, with their tremblings, their loathings, their terrors, spoke directly to my own uncertainties. *Eireball Spideoige* (A Robin's Tail), Seán Ó Ríordáin's first collection, published in 1952, was the volume that alerted me to his genius. Whoever had it before me had left greased thumbprints and yellowed tea-stains all over the book. They must have kept it in a damp place because a moist, mildewed odour came off it. Whenever I read a poem I got this sick, breathy reek as if it were coughing up its lungs in my face. That made the anguish of his TB-infested sensibilities a terrifyingly real experience for me.

Máire Mhac an tSaoi's collection, *Margadh na Saoire*, was another revelation to me. On the cover it had a delicately beautiful line drawing of a courtly lady reclining on a stylish love seat. The whole look of the book beguiled me; its shape, paper and typeface made me want to hold it, read it. The poems themselves reminded me of traditional songs, but they were infused somehow with a modern sensibility. However much they were steeped in the past, they spoke of the present. It was Gaelic singing itself confidently into the twentieth century. It was that music that got me, the vowel harmonies that flowed clear and smooth. The poems existed in the Irish language, it seemed to me, as pure sound, as speech purified, cadenced, charged.

Máirtín Ó Díreáin's slim volume of selected poems, *Rogha Dánta*, was an instant hit with me. From Inis Mór, the largest of the Aran Islands, he wrote poems that ennobled the hard struggle of his people with the land, the sea and the elements; a fierce and valiant battle that was in sharp contrast to the grey tedium of his own life as an office worker in the city. He laments an ancient way of life that is passing, with its caring, communal values, and makes plain that he is ill at ease with the self-absorbed society that is taking its place. That grieving nostalgia for a vanished past, for the lost domain of his youth, was beautifully captured in poems that were as sculpted as the faces of his islanders. Out of a bare, pared-down speech, he achieved a haunting, elemental energy that leapt off the page and caught me by the scruff of my senses. If I ever wrote poems in Irish, this approach, I thought, would be what I'd want; a fluid, flexible line that had at times the give of a good fishing-rod and at other times the stretched firmness of a fiddle-string.

Despite the lift I got from these bold, ground-breakingly modern volumes of poetry in Gaelic, I was still convinced that English would one day be my chosen vehicle of expression.

In my spare time I was writing: love poems, mostly, to those boys who excited me. So as to conceal my true feelings, these poems pretended to be about something else – a standing stone, for instance, or a hillside sapling.

I want to see your limbs tremble with light
When the earth moans in your roots;
I want to see the sap shudder in your trunk
When the sun tongues your tip;
I want to see the Spring in you
As you burst out in shoots of joy.

My poems of that time reeked of teenage lust, and in writing them I was trying to course all those gushing hormones into a spillway of words, which, instead of easing the pressure, left me dizzily unbalanced and convulsed more than ever, with a raring-to-go randiness. It was the first time I had begun to look into that terrible pool of the self. At times like that, you realise you're an abyss, a pitch-black pit. There's only a deep darkness. I got dizzy looking down into the gulf, the chasm of myself. I realised that there was an awful deadening silence . . . That there were no answers. A poem became for me an act of defiance thrown in the face of that silence.

It was also becoming clear to me that, in poetry, naming one's own private unbearable pain was not enough. You had to distance yourself from it; step back and shape it so that the purely personal experience becomes changed into a communal one. This, I was discovering, required real artistry, an imaginative negotiation with words, form and emotion. In class, we were studying Yeats and Eliot. They had it in abundance, that refined amplitude of style that was sadly lacking in my own banal attempts at poems.

I would have shown them to Mr Lally, but something in me feared they were not up to scratch, and I didn't want to bother him with my teenage trivia, my poetry of pimples. Then one day, glancing through a news magazine at school, I came across a snippet about Somerset Maugham which certainly held me back from showing my work too soon.

In the heyday of his literary fame, Maugham often received unsolicited manuscripts from aspiring writers who wanted his blessing on their work. One of these, a young, ambitious novelist who had sent him a voluminous typescript, ran into the great writer in London and with enormous self-importance asked him, 'Should I put more fire into my work?' Maugham looked him right in the eye and told him bluntly, 'No! Vice versa.' That story brought me to my senses about writing. A lot had to be discarded, I sensed, before you wrote anything of lasting value.

At the time, I was struggling to come up with a definition of
poetry that satisfied my own need for clarity and at the same time
caught something of its inexpressible elusiveness; a liberating
explanation that would elucidate rather than ensnare. As fate
would have it, I stumbled upon it in a history book. It was just a
footnote, an aside to a more pressing narrative. It concerned Lord
Norbury, an eighteenth-century Dublin judge, a hard, exacting
man with a wicked sense of humour. Once, while sentencing a
man to death for stealing a precious gold watch, he quipped, 'You
made a grab at time, idiot, but you caught eternity.' A draconian
measure for such a petty crime, however, that phrase, that
sentence could be appropriated in a more positive manner to
define poetry.

Finding that story was a sweet moment of discovery for me.
Finally, I had something that allowed me to catch what was up to
then bafflingly evasive. It was a profoundly simple idea. Poetry
makes a grasp at time but catches eternity. That means that in
spite of the shifting nature of time, poetry manages to grab
moments of passing recognition, reveal and illuminate them so
that they are captured forever.

In order to do that, I also recognised that a poet had to
cultivate what Mr Lally called 'a clear-sighted attentiveness' in
himself. If only I could do to things what the light did to them,
I would become a genuine poet, a visionary of the real. I was
enthralled by the sudden shifts of light that occur in our hilly

climate. Suddenly a hill lights up mysteriously mauve or a field glows in an amber mist or a sunset flush brightens up the face of a gloomy swamp. I wished to make poems that glowed with that light.

My mother continued her audaciously wayward journeys until I was fifteen or thereabouts at which point she became so mentally disturbed that my father had no option but 'to have her seen to, by the priest', as one holier-than-thou relative urged him to do. We tried to keep her aberrant behaviour covered up as best we could to protect her from the wagging tongues and the taunts. It wasn't easy, of course, in that rural community of the over-curious, to conceal things. The gossipmonger, the snoop and the meddler thrived in that murky climate of inquisitiveness.

It was a trying time for my father and myself. Agnes became so mentally deranged it was as if all hell had broken loose in her head and it was hugely stressful trying to cope with her. It was shocking to see her take off in a panic and shut herself away in our big solid wardrobe to escape 'the blackguards who are trying to pull the night around me neck and strangle me'.

'Who is it, Mammy?' I would enquire, terrified myself by these scary unseen presences that could pounce on you from nowhere and wipe you out in a jiffy.

'It's the bad ones from Caor an Airgid. They have it in for me,' she would whisper nervously, a strange, haunted look on her face.

'Why?'

'I know too much about the carry-on they're up to.'

I could see from the frightened, jumpy way that she peered into corners that she was scared out of her wits.

'What are they up to, Mammy?'

However much I probed her she remained tight-lipped about 'the carry-on' and would not divulge a thing.

'Go on now or I'll give you a good skite. It's not for your ears to hear what can harm you.'

It was dreadful to see her crouched anxiously inside the wardrobe or else cowering in terror under the bed. In her more alarming hysterical moods she would stalk about the house in a wicked rage, brandishing the tongs and hurling abuse at the fiends of the air. Sometimes she would stand in the doorway and leer at them with a hiss and a spit as they galloped by on their spirited white stallions.

She would peel thin wafers of flaking lime off the walls and, priest-like, raise them solemnly above her head as if consecrating communion bread while intoning with great gravity, 'Agnus Dei! Agnus Dei! Agnus Dei!' a phrase from the Mass that fascinated her because it hailed her name, she said. Often in the dead of night she would sneak out of the house if we were not wary, hardly dressed at all, and wander around the place in the raw, numbing cold, talking to herself, to the trees and to the rocks. Many a time when we went out to rescue her and cajole her back to bed we would find her prostrated in front of a hawthorn tree that grew on a grassy mound beside the house, listening, she said, to *píobaireacht as an domhan thoir*, to piping from the eastern world. At other times, we would find her by the Dúloch, the Black Lake, scrabbling about in the rushes, looking for *eochar an leasa*, the key to the *lios*, the fairy mound. One star-bright, hushed November night, the full moon dawdling above Errigal, we found her weeping uncontrollably by the well. '*Thug Domhnall na Gealaí drochiarraidh orm agus mé ag teacht trasna ón taobh eile,*' she sobbed out in distress. Domhnall, the man in the moon, had indecently assaulted her, she said, while she was coming across from the otherworld.

In the end her rages became violently abusive as she vented her fury at my father. One day when she lunged at him with a bread knife shouting, 'You're nothing but a Caor an Airgid hooligan,' he had to make a hasty run for it out the kitchen door, otherwise she would have knifed him. She was so out of control that he had to do something. He confided in a relative, a woman who spent her life pandering to the whims of the local clergy. The stench of her breath was like the clammy reek of McGeady's pigsty.

She came by one day while my father and I were keeling sheep on our outlying farm by the Dúloch. As she talked, her superior, goody-goody smugness made my blood boil.

'Poor Agnes, she's a bit touched, you know, by something . . . God forbid the thought.' She paused, and raised her yellowish, beady eyes to the sky in a gesture of affected dread. Her piety was so showy.

'Where would we be if we hadn't got our priest? The devil himself would be leapin' in us.'

The sulphurous stench of her breath reeked of hell, but I kept that to myself and managed to bear her churchy theatricality with an uneasy silence.

'Agnes should go to Mass regularly. It's a terrible thing in the eyes of God to miss the Holy Mass on a Sunday. Aye, indeed, a most grievous sin, God forgive us. I've been keeping an eye out for her but for the last five Sundays there's no styme of her to be seen.' She then turned her jaundiced eyes on me and sized me up with disdain.

It was a sultry July day. She stood there, arms crossed, beads of sweat pooling in the pitted skin of her forehead; her podgy, mealy-coloured fingers twitching on her bare upper arms like ten foraging white mice. I squirmed.

'I'll have a word with the priest himself and I'll tell him that Agnes badly needs an office to be read over her. You can be sure that he'll listen to me. Don't worry Micky, we'll get Agnes straightened out.'

The priest came on a Saturday. It must have been well into August because I recall standing by the hawthorn tree, a breezy hill wind tousling my hair and a swell of pride rising in me as I admired the ripple and sway of our pretty cornfield – a golden wave of ripening amber in the sunset – when I heard the slow rumble and hum of a car coming to a halt at the top of our lane. It was the priest in his black Morris Minor. I darted into the house to tell them that the priest had come. We could hear the sharp crunch of his confident steps as he came striding down our steep and stony laneway and suddenly, black-suited and somewhat stiff in his manner, he was standing there in our open doorway. My father, removing his old, sweaty peaked cap from his head, welcomed him to the house using the very formal, royal plural, '*tá fáilte romhaibh, taraigí isteach,*' thus showing reverence to him as a priest and homage to the Host that he may have been carrying. My father offered him a chair by the fire. There was a contrived politeness to the small talk that he and my father made about the good harvesting weather, the latest spate of deaths in the parish and the slump in the price of heifers at the local fairs. I sat on the edge of my chair, light-headed and shaky in the presence of this assured, solidly built man of God, hoping that he didn't ask me any leading questions in case I blurted out all my doubts about school and religion. But he kept aloof from me and did not in any way encourage contact.

My mother sat sullenly by the fireside and only acknowledged him with an almost imperceptible nod of her head. In the previous days she had been noticeably less frantic in her behaviour, less harried by the fury of her mania and more reasonable and coherent, by far, in her talk.

After the restrained pleasantries were done with he cleared his throat with a deep, vibrant, magisterial cough. This full-toned, flawless hawk of the throat was an authoritative signal that he was ready to begin business.

'They tell me, Agnes, that you are seeing the fairies.' He spoke with a steely firmness as if reprimanding a naughty child.

'No, Father, they're seeing me,' she shot back at him, defiantly.

I could see that he was taken aback by her lack of propriety. After all, he was a man accustomed to the doffed-cap deference of men and the 'yes, Father, if you say so' acquiescence of women. He spoke to her severely.

'You will have to stop believing in them, Agnes. Then they will not bother you any more.'

'It's more than belief, Father. Sure they're as real as you or me.' I thought it was quite plucky of her to give him the brush-off just like that.

'They're real because you believe in them,' he said, pointing his priestly finger at her threateningly.

I could see by the way she straightened up brazenly and looked him full in the face that she wasn't going to yield. My father was making an anxious dumb show of silence behind the priest's back, but she was taking no notice of his desperate antics. She smiled at the priest, a sweet, winsome smile.

'You're telling me, Father, that they are there only because I believe in them,' she said playfully. There was a mischievous glint in her eyes. At times she could be quite roguish in her humour.

'Correct! All that stuff about fairies is just a strong notion in your head. Worse still, it's a damning superstition and it has taken hold of your mind. I'm here to help you get rid of it.' As he spoke, he jutted out his sagging chin combatively and tried to lord it over her.

'If you didn't believe in God, Father, would He be there or not?' It was a crafty question asked with unabashed boldness. And it ruffled him. I watched him pull nervously at his starched, stiff collar. She was winding him up with her quick, argumentative twists and he knew it. He stood there pursing his thin lips in disgust. There was an awkward silence. I heard my father say in his quiet, pleading way, 'Now, Agnes, don't be cheeky with the priest. He's here to help you.' She ignored him completely. Instead she frowned at the priest with obvious displeasure and asked him again, but in a rather snappy manner this time.

'Tell me this, Father! If you didn't believe in God, would He be there or not?'

Her couldn't-care-less insolence flummoxed him. He took out his rosary and started fidgeting with the beads. I noticed a nervous twitch in his left eye. The poor man was in a dither. He hadn't expected to be thrown off balance by a silly, unschooled nonentity who was supposed to be soft in the head. I could see that his annoyance was gradually shifting to anger. He stood up, clattered the chair up against the table and stood over my mother, challengingly.

'Where is your faith, woman? That's an ungodly thought. The existence of God, unlike the fairies, is not something that we suppose. The existence of God is a fact.'

Having salvaged something of his wilted authority, he now paused for effect. My mother sat there, unperturbed by his rant. I could see her eyeing him up and down, dismissively, and then, before he had time to continue, she told him bluntly, with waspish scorn, 'Now! Now! Father, if there's a place for angels, surely there must be a place for fairies.' With that she rose up off the chair and with a high and mighty swagger brushed him aside and dashed off to the bedroom, laughing uproariously to herself. We could hear shrieks of laughter as she shot the bolt into place and locked the bedroom door. My father appealed to her, even implored her to open it, but there was no budging her. When the priest urged her in the name of God to open up, she burst into a hoarse, raucous delivery of 'The Wild Rover', one of the many rowdy drinking songs that she knew. My father tried to make amends to the disgruntled priest for the surly, ill-natured way that Agnes had treated him by nudging a wad of notes into what was to me an unmistakably grasping hand, however much he feigned refusal with 'You shouldn't, Micky, you shouldn't bother at all.' At the same time he was pocketing it with blatant shamelessness. I was outraged by my father squandering some of the meagre savings that he had scrimped together on this huffy, overbearing man who was supposed to have taken a vow of poverty. The money made him less grouchy and more approachable.

'I hope you'll excuse her behaviour, Father. She's a bit contrary as you see with that sickness in her head.' I didn't like my father's fawning, placatory tone and I pressed my fingers hard into my ears, but I could still hear the priest say, 'She's away with the fairies, alright, but we will get her back.' He read a few perfunctory prayers standing in the kitchen and then departed, slightly less assured, I think, than when he had arrived.

A day or two after the priest had called, Agnes collapsed to the floor one morning in a fainting fit. She was in a feverish state the night before, tossing about in the bed and sweating heavily. Micky and myself sat vigilantly by the bedside, cooling her off with a damp cloth and comforting her as best we could. We couldn't make out what she was saying but she moaned and mumbled a lot in a low, pitiful groan.

There were times that night when we thought that she wasn't going to make it to the morning. My father lit a *coinneall choisrichthe*, a blessed candle, and placed it on a chair beside the bed. He knew that I was uneasy about religion and all the ritual observances associated with it and did not make it obligatory upon me to follow suit when he knelt down to pray. Listening to him recite the Hail Mary and the Our Father out loud with conviction in that shadowy, candlelit sickroom, the rise and fall of his gravelly voice like the soothing gurgle of water around rocks, calmed my frayed nerves. I sat in silence, gripped my mother's hot, sweaty hand and asked the fairies not to take her away. I told them that I too would be at their bidding if they needed me, provided they spared her. By daybreak the worst had passed and in the morning she insisted on getting up, although she was quite shaky on her feet and slightly dopey.

She moved about the house in a daze, picking things up and addressing them in a singsong voice. She wrapped the tongs in a towel and laid it out on the table, intoning over it repeatedly, '*Mo mhaide beag briste/ a chaill a theangaidh/ I dtír idir dhá thinidh/ tá tú cliste agus níl tú cliste.*' My little broken tongs / that lost their tongue / in a country between two fires / you are smart and not so smart. Although she talked to the sooty iron kettle on the hearth, the flowery china teapot on the dresser and the blue-veiled, sad Madonna on the mantelpiece, I can only remember what she said when she hugged the ash bucket to her bosom and said over and over in a sorrowful tone, '*A bhucaid bheag na luaithe/ ná bí ar shiúl san oíche/ Bíodh ciall agat, a chroí/ is ná bí i do mháláid choíche/ aniar agus siar, aniar agus siar/ I mbéal na gaoithe.*' Little ash bucket / don't be away at night / Be steady and sensible / don't be a silly giddy biddy / back and forth, back and forth/ in the mouth of the wind.

Next, I recall her sagging to the floor and lying there comatose. My father was out in the yard sharpening a scythe. I could hear the quick stroke and scrape of the whetstone as he honed the blade to a sharp, shiny edge. I ran out in shock, shouting, 'Mammy is dying! Mammy is dying!' Micky dropped his tools instantly, blessed himself and rushed into the kitchen. He knelt down beside her, cupped her head in his big sturdy hands and nudged it gently back and forth, calling her name, 'Agnes! Agnes! Agnes!'

Suddenly her body twitched and she gasped for breath.

'That's it, Agnes, keep going. There's a struggle in you yet.'

My father was urging her in a soft, reassuring voice. Soon she was sitting up, a rumpled mess of hair and clothes. Her eyes were dull and moist. I could see her trying desperately to bring into focus the two gesturing blurs in front of her. When she spoke her voice was faint and strangely echoey as if coming from afar.

'Chuir siad an seachrán orm sna chnoic.'

They had me straying in the hills, she said, looking lost and dispirited.

The doctor came in the afternoon, a trim, well-turned-out man with a prominently noticeable gold tooth. He looked smart and dapper in his greenish tweed jacket and crisp grey trousers. With just a few polite remarks about the weather he went about his business briskly, asking searching questions about her illness. My father answered, telling him in a somewhat stiff, colourless manner about her encounters with the fairies. At this I could see the doctor nod his head knowingly and smile, a lovely charming grin that showed the full glint of his gold tooth. He then examined her thoroughly and pronounced that she was suffering from high blood pressure and, in all probability, from depression also. He wrote out a long prescription and ordered her to rest.

The drugs worked wonders in the sense that they lessened her mental agony and relieved her of those bouts of raving craziness that made our lives grim and nightmarish. Granted, they soothed and assuaged the torments that afflicted her, but they also dulled her mind, made it sluggish and inactive, numbed it so that her enchanted travels came to a halt.

My mother was reared in the old ways. The ancient belief that the otherworld was nearby and had to be given due regard was central to the world-view of the culture that shaped her.

She was brought up in a world of portents and omens; where the omnipresent dead sent warnings and signals; where certain birds were harbingers of misfortune or even heralds of death; where sometimes a ghostly cortège appeared out of nowhere and passed through mournfully into the unseen. That world impressed itself so strongly upon her mind that it became for her an indisputable fact, a living, tangible reality, clear as daylight.

It was, of course, a world that ran foul of the Catholic Church of the time because it provided an alternative spirituality: an ancient, deeply indigenous pantheism. The Church of that era was a highly aggressive, control-obsessed establishment and could not countenance the challenge of such a compelling visionary faith.

Furthermore, in a world that was rapidly changing, the old folk ways with their easy familiarity with the preternatural were giving way to a more hard-headed, pragmatic understanding of things. The fairy faith became a quaint, bygone notion.

'The electric light killed off the fairies' was how the locals summed up this shift in thinking.

My mother was a mystic in her own right. She surprised me many times, with her bright, intuitive perceptions, that is, before the drugs took their toll and blunted her intensely sensitive mind.

One hot Sunday afternoon in June, while we were having the usual packet soup and spuds dinner, she said, as she was ladling out the over-boiled broth, 'I was wakened up this morning by the scent of a wee yellow flower that's growin' yonder in the hedge.'

'How did you know it was yellow?' I asked her teasingly, trying to outmanoeuvre her.

'It had a yellow smell, that's why.'

One wet April evening, the air heady with the steamy reek of new growth, we were idling in the doorway, when, suddenly, a thrush burst into song on a nearby tree, delighting us with its pure ineffable trill of joy. She stood there, visibly moved by that sheer soar of bliss. After a minute or two of silence, she turned to me and said excitedly, 'Sometimes, you know, when I hear a thrush sing like that, I step out of myself.'

Another time we were sitting under the old ash tree by the henhouse admiring a very fiery sunset that made the glen glow with an intense rose light when she observed, 'D'you ever notice old trees? There's always a very still, yellowy-green light around them. It's more calming to sit under them than it is to sit under young trees. Young trees have a whirlin' red light around them. They make you dizzy.'

Now I like to think of my mother more as a rustic mystic than as somebody 'with a wild, bad dose of the nerves'. But, perhaps these two conditions are complementary, or, indeed, one and the same. Anyway, they do characterise someone who has a hyper-sensitivity, an acute intuitiveness to the multiple dimensions of reality. That was my mother before the sedatives desensitised her mind.

Puberty, that rancid hormonal surge that convulsed my body at twelve, left me gaping at boys instead of girls. I wanted to press myself against their groins, kiss their shadowy moustaches, squeeze their rounded buttocks. At the tech, boys in my class were themselves in the throes of change. Breathing in the fetid odour of sex that came off them left me reeling.

There was a boy with soft, luscious eyes who sat with me sometimes in class. He was sixteen. I was a year older than him. I'd nudge his leg with my hand and if he didn't pull back, I'd rub it slowly until I felt it twitch and yield. He'd slide forward in the chair and part his legs so that I could feel and knead the full of his thigh. He always wore light, baggy pants which, when the mast was raised, bellied out like a sail in the wind. Whenever his stiff became unbearable, he'd take off his jacket and lay it across his lap. That was the signal for me to sneak my hand underneath and touch it.

Ever so gently, I'd fondle its tip as it rose and dipped, rose and dipped. We wouldn't look at each other or speak, we'd just sit there and keep our faces impassive while, below, we were riding the waves of joy.

He was the first boy I saw in the nip. One Sunday in May, I agreed to go walking with him to Loch na Cuiscreach, a lonely, tucked-away lake in the bogs beyond my house. It was a hot day; on the turf banks, soft brown sods were hardening in the sun. He brought along two oranges which we ate, spread out in the heather by the lake. That day the light on distant hills had the same yellow succulence as the juice that dripped off our chins.

Beads of sweat glistened on his brow. He wore a mousy-coloured peaked cap which belonged to his uncle, he said, a cheap orange gansey and old jeans frayed at the knees and grimy where they fitted into his turned-down wellingtons. He didn't give two hoots about clothes and couldn't understand my fussy tastes. He had a household of older brothers and wore, mostly, their scruffy hand-me-downs. These stained, worn-out bits and pieces gave him, in my eyes, a rakish, tinker-boy look that excited me. As if he lived in the wilds, out beyond the norms.

'I'm taking a dip,' he said. 'I'm roasting.' And, natural as anything, he stripped down to his loose, blue underpants. 'Come on, it's warm,' he shouted back to me as he waded out into the lake. He took easily to the water and could even swim a little, whereas I was completely out of my depth in it. As well as that, I was ashamed of my puny muscles and my lack of colour. My skin was sickly pale and looked as if I had pulled a strip of bandage off it.

Nevertheless, the sight of him, his bare sinewy body ribbed and corded like a wee ship rigged out with ropes, emboldened me. Wearing only my dark patterned shorts, I stepped out, teeth chattering, and stood up to my knees in the shivery water. Playfully, he bobbed up and down and made choppy waves around me. The taut cordage of muscle which rippled beautifully when he moved made me breathless and I had to sit down in the water to conceal my excitement.

I wanted to hold him close; be buoyed up by him and enjoy the plunge and thrash of our bodies as we drifted together, joined at the groin. But we kept our distance. While he swam about I skimmed flat stones across the water to keep calm.

When he'd had enough of sloshing about in the lake he came

out, radiantly wet; wriggled himself out of his dripping undies and lay in the raw on cushiony tufts of moss by the water. At first some awkward diffidence kept me away from him, but I couldn't keep myself in check for long and slipped down beside him. He lay on his back, eyes closed, arms by his sides. A shiny rivulet of hairs ran from the bright, fleecy lake between his legs up to the dark drop of his bellybutton. His skin had an oatmeal pastiness except where the sun had touched his face and neck and arms, and there it had a gypsy brown ruddiness about it.

He wasn't a pretty boy, not even moderately handsome. He had a heavy, clumsy face as if the features were an afterthought, lumpy add-ons that had no regard for comeliness. Other than two dewy eyes that sparkled, his face was unremarkable. It was his body that astonished me; when he was covered up, I never suspected that he was this tight-knit, brawny specimen, already a man in the loins. Lying on my side, facing him, I pressed against his hip and delicately manoeuvred my leg across his and then sank into a feigned sleep. I heard him shift his head towards me and felt the creep of his breath, like the gentlest touch imaginable, on my chest. I yearned for this moment of closeness to go on and on, this companionable stillness where I breathed in unison with another being.

A lark let loose its tumult of joy above us; a stray breeze passed over us, laden with the scent of heather. How lovely it would be, I thought, to spend the night out here with this boy, the spongy earth underneath us, the glittery blanket of the heavens above us, and the two of us, swaddled in this easy contentment.

I felt him stir, turn and face me and then he was on top of me, deep and needy in his moves. 'Take a hoult of it,' he urged and I did, slotting my hand around it tightly so that he could hole his thrusts. He groaned, eased himself off me and lay face down in the moss. My ears buzzed, I flushed, I felt weak with the excitement of it and yet there was something amiss. He never touched my privates, never even bothered to slip down my undies, never mouthed me in any way.

'Do you like me?' I asked him and ran my fingers through the hairy cleft of his arse.

'Get away out of that with ye,' he grinned up at me. 'I'm not a nancy boy.'

'And what are you?' I asked irritably.

He stood up, brushed away the wisps of moss that got stuck in his pubic hairs and laughed: 'I'm just horny and waiting for the real thing.' He looked down at his shrivelled penis and patted it. 'I'm promising this footy wee thing that he's going to get it soon.'

'Didn't he get it just now?' I spoke severely. How could he dismiss what we had done?

'You must be joking,' he retorted bluntly. 'You can only get it with girls.' I seethed with anger but managed to restrain myself.

Making an issue of it was, I decided, no good. At any rate I wasn't ready to reveal myself yet and angry, unguarded words would surely lead to disclosures. 'Oh!' I remarked drily.

We dressed and out of a curt politeness walked a little way together. Where our paths forked, he took the main road and I wandered off down a tangled lane of gorse. As the evening came on, the light on distant hills paled into a lovely ooze of pink and lavender that slowly dripped down into the bogs and across the fields.

We were never close again. We spoke but it was strained. Every word had a jagged edge. Our easy, fumbling, wordless intimacy was gone. Shame bristled between us like a stretch of barbed wire.

I have never been in the closet. I say that because we never had
anything as fashionably snazzy as a closet in our house. It's more
likely that I was in the *lios*, the abode of the fairies. By sixteen,
I came to accept that I was gay. It was an unspoken
understanding with myself. It wasn't the Holy Spirit flaring up
in me in a Pentecostal bringing to light; no, it was simply that
I had a chance encounter with a book. Literature lured me out
of the *lios*.

It was Gore Vidal's *The City and the Pillar*, which my father
picked up at random in Glasgow and brought in the big sack of
books which he always carried back to me. At the time, it was
a godsend, an unlooked-for testament of hope and promise. It
was the first time I had read about a romance between two men
in a book, and, although their relationship was a tortured one,
frightened and doomed to failure, it was an acknowledgement
of the public reality of homosexuality. For me, a young
adolescent in the wilds of Donegal, coming to terms with my
sexual difference, it was an assurance, a guarantee even, that I
wasn't on my own. Out there, somewhere, were others of a
similar bent. That gave me a mighty shot of self-confidence and
cockiness. My falling in love with boys rather than with girls
was, I realised, nothing more than a biological predilection.
A*bum*inable I may be, it occurred to me at the time, but not
abominable.

It was then that I started in earnest to look out for, and read,
authors who confessed their gayness in their writings. There

were hardly any bookshops in Donegal and certainly none that catered for my particular needs. I had to look elsewhere. The summer before I sat for my Leaving Certificate I worked in a north Dublin hotel and the following summer, soon after finishing exams, I got a job in a hotel in County Wicklow, an hour or so by bus from Dublin. This allowed me to trawl the city-centre bookstores: Webb's, Parsons, the Eblana, Greene's, and find and pleasure myself with Oscar Wilde's *The Picture of Dorian Grey*, Christopher Isherwood's *Goodbye to Berlin*, André Gide's *The Immoralist*, James Baldwin's *Giovanni's Room* and the poetry of Walt Whitman. By putting together this bookish who's who of homos, I felt I was being initiated into a gay fraternity of literature. Walt Whitman vowed that he would plant male friendships thick as trees along the riverbanks of America. I knew that he was talking to me directly when he said:

> I mind once how we lay such a transparent summer morning
> How you settled your head athwart my hips
> And gently turned over upon me
> And parted the shirt from my bosom bone
> And placed your tongue to my bare stripped heart
> And reached till you felt my beard
> And reached till you held my feet

That poem was a mighty assuring yes to my condition. At a local charity sale, I came across a copy of Tennessee Williams' *The Glass Menagerie* and bought it. 'What is straight?' a character asks and the response is, 'A line can be straight, or a street, but the human heart, oh no! It curves like a road through mountains.' I understood that perfectly. The Donegal mountain roads were quite bent.

The Catholicism that I got at primary school was dour and dark; sex was serpent-energy, where the devil inserted his horn into my dick and made it sinfully rigid. If I touched it I was fondling the devil. One day in my final year, a schoolmate told me that he had had a strange experience the night before. He'd rubbed his dick too roughly and the devil had spat at him. He enjoyed it, he said, but was terribly frightened because he must have hurt and angered the devil with his rough handling. I reassured him that anything that hurt the devil was good, positively good. I then suggested that we would hurt the devil together.

And we did. Over the next few weeks, we walloped the devil every chance we got, so much so that he could barely spit in the end. We became deft hands at the emissionary position, that is, until my friend told me rather brusquely that he would much prefer to have a girl share the experience rather than me.

I was lucky in the sense that my mother's faith in the fairy world had a stronger formative and shaping effect on me than Catholicism ever had. After all, I became a 'fairy' myself.

As a young child, I was awe-struck by the grandeur and the solemnity of certain Catholic ceremonies: the Midnight Mass; the Benedictions; the funeral services. The colourful vestments left me gaping, the smell of incense had me in a swoon. Later, as a teenager at the tech, I became appalled at the dogma, the unyielding, harsh canonical tenets that tried to instil in me a terrible sense of shame and guilt about who and what I was. If I fell prey to guilt, I knew that they could easily control me. So I didn't. Love for my fellow men was, I discovered, a pleasure too keen to forgo even with the promise of paradise. Anyway, paradise, as I saw it, was not a place but a position: being joined at the loins with another boy, in joy. I was not going to be branded. I was not going to be confused by labels. Religion, I realised, was extremely wily at making a ceremony of death out of the miracle of life.

A friend of mine told me a joke at the time about a man who couldn't stop wanking. This sinful activity worried him so much that he decided to go to the local priest, a grave, elderly man of great piousness, to get his advice and counsel. Was it acceptable, he asked the priest, to masturbate while he was praying? The old wise priest frowned and told him that it wasn't − but he paused, reflected and then added, 'It's wickedly sinful to masturbate while you are praying but it might be less so if you tried to pray while you masturbated.' The joke beautifully illustrated the fact that you could transgress if only you knew the right theological loophole. That was a heartening realisation.

Anyway, I was getting high on expansiveness be it in pop or in poetry. I was into the bliss business of Eastern beliefs. Karma appealed to me more than dogma.

After all, it was the sixties and I was getting an earful of its vibrations from the radio. Musically, I was weaned on Radio Luxembourg. In the evenings, I would nuzzle up to our little transistor and let that fantastic ferment of sixties sounds flow through me. This music provided the soundtrack to my sexual awakening. Songs like Amen Corner's 'Bend Me, Shape Me', Dusty Springfield's 'I Don't Know What to Do with Myself', Herman's Hermits' 'I'm into Something Good', Steppenwolf's 'Born to be Wild', Manfred Mann's 'Doo Wah Diddy Diddy', The Kinks' 'Lola', The Equals' 'Baby Come Back' and Procol Harum's 'A Whiter Shade of Pale' were, for me, sexual liberation songs. The Top Twenty was more pertinent to my salvation than the Ten Commandments.

In the early sixties, John Charles McQuaid, the then dourly conservative archbishop of Dublin, stated after returning from a Vatican Two meeting, 'There has been much talk of change.

Let me reassure you that no change will disturb the tranquillity of your Catholic lives.' As a stern establishmentarian of the old order, he opposed the radical shake-up of the Church proposed by that progressive Council. Despite the reactionary rhetoric of McQuaid and his ilk, the country was loosening up. The mini-skirt saw to that. As hemlines were being raised, sexual scruples were slackening.

De Valera's rural arcadia, that dreary monochrome ideal of comely maidens and stalwart youths dancing at the crossroads, was gone. A lounge bar permissiveness was taking the place of the dry parish hall dances. The showbands were in full swing. The encouragingly bright economic policies of Lemass were giving the Ireland of the mid-sixties a little bit of technicolour vibrancy.

There was a noticeable burgeoning of prosperity in our area, not so much from any local boom, but from the money earned on well-paid building sites in England and Scotland. People were beginning to rig out their homes with electrical mod-cons, cookers and kettles, fridges and toasters. Piped water and indoor loos were the in thing.

My father, when he went to Scotland, no longer worked on the farms but stayed with Auntie Biddy in Ballater Street and laboured on roadworks and building sites in Glasgow. With the money he made, we replastered the house, replaced the windows and repaired the roof. An ostentatious 'kitchen cabinet' with sliding glass doors and a wee pull-out table dislodged the dresser. The wide open hearth gave way to a built-up, raised iron grate. However, unlike many of the older houses, where the walls were glossed up with 'beauty board' and the flagstones were clad with 'linoleum', we still limewashed our walls and left our flagstones uncovered.

We drew our own water from the well, still used the outside

lavatory and had no television. But we had books, heaps of them, thanks to my father who bought them second-hand in Glasgow and always came home loaded with two or three sacks crammed with a mix of titles. His random pickings allowed me to read about life in the city states of ancient Greece, the fall of the Roman Empire, the Crusades, Buddhism and the path to enlightenment, the pygmies of the Congo jungle, the War of the Roses, the Reformation in Europe, wild flowers of the British Isles and the Hopi Indians and their beliefs. Thomas Hood, Francis Thompson, Walter de la Mare, Edith Sitwell, Wilfred Owen, Vachel Lindsay, Ezra Pound, Robert Service, W.H. Auden, William Wordsworth, John Keats, Edward Thomas were the poets that he brought to me. The list of fiction is too long to enumerate but included authors like John Steinbeck, Ernest Hemingway, Boris Pasternak, Compton McKenzie, Zane Grey, Lewis Carroll, Gore Vidal, E.M. Forster, Hermann Hesse, Jack Kerouac and Mark Twain.

These books raised me out of rural isolation and allowed me to enter multiple worlds of experience, thus broadening my mind to other cultures, to other valid and varied ways of seeing and thinking about the world I lived in.

At the tech, Mr Lally, a great encourager of ideas and a disseminator of them too, would give over a class entirely to debate; an open forum for free thinking on a wide range of topics. Should we legalise contraception, allow divorce, decriminalise homosexuality, abandon religion, adopt socialism? Should there be women priests? We discussed mini-skirts and Women's Lib, unmarried mothers, censorship, the Cold War and a whole lot of other current social issues.

He introduced us to the psychedelic concepts of love-in and be-ing and all the tuned-in buzz words of that hallucinogenic decade: dope, turned on, trip, stoned, high, spaced out. We wrote essays on 'Flower Power', 'Does Free Love Really Free Us Up', 'Jesus Was the First Hippy', 'The Idea of a Commune'. He tried to inculcate in us a sense of the liberating times that we lived in so that we would be better equipped to benefit from them. Fortunately for him and for us, the tech was not under the oppressive thumb of the Church. If it had been, the liberal bountifulness of his teaching would not have been tolerated. In this truly secular space, Mr Lally created a free zone of thinking – a bold, Haight-Ashbury of our own in the Bay Area of Gortahork – that gave me and my classmates much latitude to develop.

In my final year at the tech, I wrote a batch of poems in Gaelic inspired by Michael Davitt and Gabriel Rosenstock, two young contemporary poets whose work was causing a bit of a stir in the Irish-language literary world. One of these poems, '*Boitheach na Bó*', would be my first bit of published writing.

Michael Davitt was a tuned-in, amped-up, streetwise cosmopolitan who set the fads, the lingo, the stances. I loved the sounds he made, the jazzy urgency of his style that made Gaelic go be-bop in the night with a swinging, snazzy self-confidence. Davitt was a child of the sixties, a freewheelin' follower of the new vision, a believer in that costumed counter-culture that put a rosy glow in the mind and a rainbow show in the wardrobe. He brought all of that expanded-mind exuberance to bear on the writing of poetry in the Irish language. He took me out in the carefree caravan of his poetry to a lovely mellow yellow domain somewhere between Dylan and Dun Caoin.

Likewise, the poetry of Gabriel Rosenstock was dashingly cool and daringly hip. Their dialogue with other cultures, their impish humour, their openness to the unexpected made his poems hugely appealing. The poetry of Davitt and

Rosenstock were, for me, messages in a bottle from a distant *Tír na nÓg*, a revitalised, groovy, Gaelic Ireland that flourished defiant and free on the margins of English. I had found my role models.

I am not the first man of letters from our area. That distinction goes to Dinny Mhicí Dhonncaidh of Gortbán who for a decade or so pursued his epistolary zeal and wrote outrageously kinky letters to local women, especially those whose husbands were away working in Scotland.

Dinny was naturally skilled and could turn a hand to anything; an able carpenter, a gifted creel maker, a clever jeweller who shaped shiny rings out of the rims of shilling coins and, as it turned out, an inspired but warped hewer of words.

As a child, I watched him weave and plait sally rods into a springy latticework of green. He worked, teeth gritted in stubborn silence, and became narky if anyone distracted him. I admired the exquisite skill he had in threading and twisting those soft, lissome willows into the tight interweave that became, after a day or two of slow, meticulous work, a strong, bouncy, reed-smelling turf creel.

I was allowed to watch from a distance but never encouraged to lend a hand to the handiwork, however much I yearned to bend and braid those pliant rods into a mess of green. If I stepped too close while he worked, he stopped me in my tracks with a few nasty grunts.

He loathed chatty neighbours who came by for a natter when he was working, and had no qualms about telling them to eff off. On a gusty July afternoon, turf-gathering time, Micky, a rather jolly, laid-back bletherer, came by while Dinny was repairing an old wooden turf barrow outside his house. Micky flopped down beside Dinny on an outcrop of rock, pulled a packet of Players from the back pocket of his mucky corduroys, and was about to launch into his usual gossipy yap when Dinny stared at him grimly and snarled, 'I've no time to waste on slack loafers like you.' With that, he turned his back on Micky and set to work promptly, nailing the loose laths of the wheelbarrow with renewed vigour, leaving the neighbour to sneak away, quietly.

Dinny was like that, a rude misfit with no sense of neighbourly decorum. Much as I admired his skills, I never warmed to him. There was something chilling about him, like the scary tree I saw from the window of the bus on that day I went to my grandmother's house in Mín Doire na Slua. It had been charred by lightning and it spooked me. On the way back, I avoided looking at it. Dinny disturbed me in that same uncanny way. His swarthy face had the look of scorched wood.

Most of the local men took little heed of their posture. They slouched about with droopy shoulders and slightly stooped backs. Dinny was an exception. He always stood and walked bolt upright, head and shoulders thrown back aggressively in a severe and heavy pose. Most of the time he was standoffish and sullen. When he spoke there was something knotty in the strained hesitations of his speech as if each word was a small, gnarled lump that had to be forced though a raw and inflamed throat. He wasn't at all talkative except once in a while when he spoke to himself. Then he raged, a furious outburst as if rounding on himself, lashing out at some insufferable inner self, berating and scolding it viciously.

One time I came upon him unawares while he talked to himself at the well below his house. He didn't know that I was jouking in the whins behind him, watching his every move. He held up the lapel of his jacket, stuffed his head inside and fumed at some unseen presence. 'Didn't I tell you to stop that, you silly cunt. You're showing me up.' A lot of what he said was indistinct and fitful and sounded just like the jerky garbled reception that we got on our old box radio.

He lived with two brothers and a sister, all single, in a bleak, soulless bungalow in Gortbán, a mile or so from our house. Unlike the other houses in the neighbourhood that glowed with a homely charm – bright patterned oilcloth on the table, floral curtains at the windows, a rose bush by the door – Dinny's house was a cold, forbidding place. It wasn't rundown or shabby. They cared for it and kept it austerely neat. But there was a strangely stark look about the place. I used to think that it had an angry stare, that it scowled at me and discouraged any cosy familiarity.

Inside was as cold and featureless as the outside. On the rare occasion that I had to go in on some errand or other, I felt on edge. A chilly draught creaked through the house as if some spectral presence stalked the place. A sluggish turf fire smoked on the kitchen hearth, but I never saw that smouldering heap of sods burst into a welcoming blaze. It burned with a slow hiss and a crackle; a dampened flicker now and then but never that flaming red-hot radiance that I was used to at home.

They had no idea of colour coordination either. Even a child could see that. They painted the upper part of the kitchen walls in a deep, murky cream and the lower half a glum, sallow green. Above all of that was a flat cocoa-coloured raftered ceiling. There was a blue Formica-covered table with three glossy brown chairs by the curtainless window. That was the only heart-warming shininess in the place, a little cheerful gleam in an otherwise dour kitchen.

The sister, Kitty, sat on a bench-like long stool by the fire, rocking to and fro; a dowdy huddle in black, humming snatches of Gaelic songs to herself. She, like the fire, burned without a sparkle. At the time, I heard someone say on the radio that the eyes were the windows of the soul. Once when I called in to sell raffle tickets I looked into her eyes and they were listless and scummy as if boarded up, like the windows of abandoned houses in the area whose families had left their harsh, peaty hill farms for good and gone off to better prospects, they hoped, in Scotland. Living in such dark conditions without an outlet to the light, I thought her soul must be deathly pale like the wan, whitish grass that sometimes grew inside those deserted houses.

Once, though, I must have been nine at the time, she came to life, unexpectedly, in a blaze of passion. The social welfare officer or 'gauger' as that *persona non grata* was dubbed in West Donegal in those economically severe times came to the house to means-test one of the brothers who had applied for the dole. Kitty fell for this blond, boyishly lean government official and imagined that he was her boyfriend. She would sit by the roadside in front of her house for hours on end, all dolled up in a tight pea-green dress that smelled of camphor and mothball, waiting for her imaginary suitor to come and take her away.

'I'm waiting for the gauger. He's taking me with him,' she would say, breathlessly, when the neighbours walked by. The neighbours, of course, to and froed the road tirelessly. They were all agog with the reckless, dotty romance. They knew right well that it had no real substance to it other than in Kitty's own stirred-up imagination.

'I'm the lucky girl to be getting a big shot,' she said to my mother, when we met her one day on our way to Annie Bharney's shop in Baltony.

'I'll be living in a big house in Letterkenny. Just ask for Mrs McGinty the gauger's wife and they'll know where I am.'

And she was off, swanking it up the road in her arched, strapped, high-heel shoes, an ear-to-ear smile encircling her puffed and jowly moon face.

During the months of her bright-eyed watch, she was a woman with a purpose in life. I couldn't but notice the change that came over her. It was as if she had been set alight from within. She was a vivacious blaze of energy, vividly alive. Her long-faced scowl was replaced by a lovely sparkling smile. She even became a little comely.

Occasionally, one or other of the brothers would roar at her from the yard while she patrolled the road in front of the house.

'Get in here you good-for-nothing eejit and do something.'

One evening I saw her struggling with two of them as they shoved and prodded her like a cow up the pathway to the house. They had her hands clasped tightly behind her back. She was powerless in their big, burly grip as they pushed her in the front door.

'You'll have us in the papers with your fuckin' capers,' one of them was bawling at her.

Despite being picked on and pushed around, she kept her romantic vigil by the roadside with impeccable composure. This all-out ardour lasted about five months. Then she realised that the man she longed for was not coming to take her away.

She came to our house one muggy midsummer's afternoon. A lush heaviness lay over everything. She was in an awful, tearful state. She paced up and down the kitchen floor sobbing and wouldn't sit, flailing her gangly arms in a gesture of hopelessness.

'He's gone, gone, gone!'

Her oily face was splodged with patches of poorly applied powder. When she cried, the tears streaked down her cheeks and made this smudgy make-up drip off her jowls like candle grease.

'This'll surely send me to me grave.'

'Will ya whist,' my mother said. 'Don't be talking about dyin'. Be talkin' about dancin'.'

Her make-up had become by now a glossy blight, a furry decay that blotched her face.

'I'll never get over him.'

Her tiny pale eyes reminded me of unhatched eggs left to rot in a nest.

'What under God's name did he say to you anyway that you're so stuck on him?' my mother asked her.

'He said nothing. He just looked at me and, I swear to God, Agnes, all of me went into a wild jiggle.'

'He looked at you? That's all?' my mother said, incredulously.

'That look was enough, Agnes.'

They looked at each other enquiringly and I saw a suggestive smile pass between them.

'Ah hah!' My mother nodded her head knowingly. 'You've got the hots for him alright.'

'You couldn't souse it, Agnes, if you were to throw Dúloch over me.'

They laugh, a giddy, girlish laugh. I keep my eyes averted and stare at a fury of flames rising up in the fireplace.

''Tis a pity you didn't have a right wee tumble with him,' my mother joked.

'Anyway, he's not the only man in the world,' she said, in a loud effusive voice.

'He's the only man in my world.'

I could hear the moan in Kitty's voice.

'Here, a wee sup of tea. It'll do you the world of good.'

My mother handed her a mug of tea. It shook and spilled over a little in her unsteady hands. I watched her put it to her lips, slobber over it and cool it with a breathy hiss. She slopped five spoonfuls of sugar into it, tasted it with a loud slurp, and smacked her lips with satisfaction.

'That's it, *a thaisce*, put a wee spoonful of hope into your cup of life and you'll be doing grand.' My mother was patting her gently on the back.

'He's the only man in me world and the fuckin' lout has left me heart sore.'

Her bitterness shone bright as the red brooch pinned to the collar of her green cardigan.

My mother buttered her a chunk of oven-fresh bread.

'I'll never get a man. Never.' She swirled her head so that her thick jet-black hair fell in a waving swell around her face. In the glow of the fire it was full of glints and gleams like the changing hues of duck feathers on a rainy day. I thought it was beautiful. I thought, if some man saw her like this, her dappled hair would attract him. I felt sorry for her.

'You won't get one cryin'.' My mother spoke to her in a breezy manner. 'You'll have to go out there, girl, and be like a hoor at a crossroads.'

'Aye! Aye! Aye!' she kept saying. It sounded lonely and despairing. My mother put her arms around her and stroked her hair.

I slipped out of the doorway. In the purple dusk the rich fragrance of rose filled the yard. I saw the sun stroking the back of the evening hills. They almost swelled to that touch. I knelt down by the well and prayed to the Virgin Mary that our Kitty would get a man.

Back in 1963, something happened that made me even more wary of Dinny than before. It was a severe winter, one of the worst on record in our area. Below-zero nights and bright snowbound days made life difficult for the hill-farming community. Cattle had to be confined to byres, watered and foddered for days on end. Sturdy black-faced sheep that usually fended for themselves on a vast acreage of hillside commonage had to be penned in walled gardens or else shielded in hastily made shelters.

Mín A Leá was deep in snow and brimming with light. The lie of the land changed. It became uncharted countryside. Hills and hollows were obliterated by this weighty bulk of brilliance that fell from the sky. It was a boy's world. I loved its blank dazzle, a boundless white page of possibilities that didn't cramp you like the lined pages in my school exercise book. Here there were no enforced limits, no cruel teacher to curb a flight of fancy.

I realised that I had to carry a similar unbounded sweep of space inside my mind if I were to survive the stifling confines of my schooling. It was exhilarating to watch a honking V of wild geese flying overhead. I imagined that the V had mitched from the rigid school of the alphabet and was now out on its own on an airy romp across those unsettled wintry skies. I would be sad when the snow thawed. Then everything would be back again to its usual geography of greyness. I must, I pledged to myself, maintain a snowland in my mind.

That winter, the entire neighbourhood became one huge field

that was raked daily by a barbed brush of white wind. The Dúloch was frozen, a thick black slab of slipperiness, beneath a dusting of snow. Everybody said that it was extremely dangerous to go out on it, but that made it all the more exciting.

One dusk, when there was nobody about, I ventured out, skidding and skating. I was halfway across when I heard the clonk of cracking ice. Long streaks of white, like the clawing nails of some underwater monster, cracked across the black glassy surface. I was terrified that it would open its icy maw and gulp me up. I could hear the slosh and slap of water when I moved. My heart was thumping wildly like the starling I had snared the day before and held briefly in my hand. The twitch of fear in its frail body and the nervous pounding of its heart made me pity it. I let it loose. Now I was glad that I had let it go. Didn't my mother always say that a good deed was like money put aside for an emergency. It was a guarantee in a time of crisis. It bailed you out of danger, she said. Now I needed all the surety I had stashed away to get me out of harm's way. I must have enough good deeds credited to my account by now, I hoped, to get me out of this bother.

What about the time last spring when I came upon a neighbour's lamb badly entangled in briars and in cutting it free scratched and gashed my hands and cheeks. For weeks afterwards I bore those red weals like a raw map of pain on my face and didn't make a fuss about it, and, unlike the other boys, I didn't mock my classmate who left a steaming pool of piss at his feet when the teacher walloped him for misspellings. Suddenly there was a hissing split where I stood. I crept on all fours to spread my weight more evenly, inching my way as best I could out of those gaping cracks.

I heard someone laugh. It was then that I noticed Dinny, standing on the opposite bank, his hands stuck in his pockets, laughing. I was on my hands and knees testing the ice for firmness when there was a loud smash. A slab of ice gave way at my feet and I felt the deadly chill of water lodging in my wellingtons.

'Help me, Dinny,' I screamed at him. I was shaking. I waited to hear a kindly voice that would soothe me, buoy me up and guide me to safety. He just stood there and teased me.

'Do you hear that crack? You're for the big plunge, boy.'

By this time I was crying unashamedly, great gulping sobs, but the more I cried the louder he guffawed.

'You're lucky you can't swim. You'll drown quicker when you go under,' he jeered.

He was willing to let me drown. That unnerved me. I looked around in despair. Errigal was snuffed out in a thick grey swathe of cloud. Drowning must be like that, I guessed. A terrible smothering as bales of water are bundled down your throat. Thinking about it made me gasp for breath.

In the distance I could hear my father harangue the dogs. He was foddering the sheep in the field by the river. It was a voice from the faraway land of the living. At that moment I felt Death taking hold of me, grasping me in its icy grip. I knew the land of the dead was a land of chilly silence. I touched my grandfather's face as he lay in his coffin and it was icy cold and silent. Death, I guessed then, was some ghostly force that came to freeze us up forever. Now I felt a numbness sneaking into my toes, and slithering up my fingers. I shivered. Death had begun to enter me . . .

If someone threw me a rope I would be saved.

'Go down and tell Daddy to get a rope,' I yelled at Dinny.

'You want to hang yourself, do you?' he shot back at me with glee. Then he sauntered off casually up the back road, away from the houses. He left me to drown.

That focused me. I was getting out of this alive, I told myself. For the sake of Micky and Agnes, I had to survive. If I drowned they would be left childless. I couldn't bear to think of the grief that would cause them.

Slowly, slowly I retreated and found myself on solid ice. I crept to the safety of the shore.

After that I shunned Dinny, and refused to speak to him. Oddly enough, he always greeted me whenever we met as though nothing untoward had happened. I couldn't understand how he could be so callous and then so civil. He must, I sensed, be cut off from his feelings. Occasionally he would visit us, usually at night. 'I'm out for a dander,' he would say, 'and here I am.'

'Here you are,' my mother would say, scathingly, 'when you should be someplace else.'

He didn't notice the scorn in her voice or else ignored it.

'I get so bored with that dour Dinny fella that pissin' sounds exciting,' my mother would say. His back to the fire, he'd hunker down, feet wide apart and warm his rump over the blaze.

'If you stand in that heat any longer that rubbery arse of yours will melt and suffocate the lot of us. I'm gettin' the fumes already.' My mother couldn't stand him. In his own good time he'd sit down and shuffle about restlessly on a creaking wooden chair by the kitchen bed until he found the most agreeable position to sprawl out in and at the same time the best vantage point to stare at us. He'd stay stretched out like that for about an hour without saying much, just the occasional 'I see' or 'Aye! Aye!'

On his way out he'd scan the stack of books that were piled on the dresser, leaf through any that took his fancy and usually select one to take home.

'I'll take this one with me,' he'd say in a strong, proprietorial tone. He never returned a book of his own accord. My father had to go and demand them back and even then it was difficult to get them off him. We had a big, heavy, gold-embossed, green-covered book of Greek myths that he coveted. He took this book three or four times and we had to keep nagging at him for weeks to bring it back. I wondered at the time why he had such a pressing need of this volume. Eventually he assumed ownership of it. Trying to retrieve books from him became a tiresome ordeal. In the end we became resigned to the fact that he wasn't going to return certain books. At that point we moved all our books to the bedroom so that he wouldn't have access to them and refused flatly to lend him any more. Little did we know at the time that our books had an enormous bearing on his letter writing.

Nora John, our next-door neighbour, came to our door, flushed and out of breath. 'Dinny has been nicked,' she blurted out in a wheeze of excitement. 'The gardaí were at the house just now and they hauled him off to the barracks in Falcarragh.'

'What's he done?' my father asked, stunned by the news. To be arrested and taken into custody was a momentous event in our area. It occurred to me that Dinny must have snapped and done away with his sister. I knew that he had that threatening, shadowy side to him.

'He's been sendin' filthy letters to women all over the place for years,' Nora said. 'Sure I've got heaps of them myself.'

'Filthy letters!' my father said, astonished.

'He was talking shite in all of them, but some, mind you, was far dirtier than that.'

I was disappointed. I expected some brutal murder or at least a savage assault in which he had gouged out somebody's eye with an awl. A gut-churning, blood-soaked story was what I expected. But letter writing sounded so tame, so unexciting.

'I didn't know he had a dirty mind like that,' my father said.

'It's not a mind he has, Micky, but a fuckin' midden. God forgive me for cursin'!'

'I didn't get any of his letters,' my mother said, sheepishly.

'There was no point in sending you a letter, Agnes,' my father said, 'you couldn't read a word of it.'

'I didn't know meself the big baloney words he used,' Nora said, 'but I knew they were drippin' with dirt.'

Nora told us that a local woman went to the gardaí in Falcarragh and lodged a complaint about the nasty mail she was getting. The gardaí took her bundle of offensive letters and checked out the handwriting against signatures on all the dole slips from the area. Dinny's signature matched the scribble in the letters and he was nabbed.

Following his arrest many women in the area spoke out and admitted that they too had got 'dirty letters' on a regular basis. For about ten years Dinny had pursued his epistolary pesterings without hindrance. The letters always came, they said, when their husbands were away working in Scotland. They put up with them because they were too shy and ashamed to do otherwise. They were repulsively personal but, worse still, they were often too close to the bone on family matters that were deemed to be private. That, of course, created a sense of tense suspicion in the locality. Every woman who got the letters was on the lookout for telltale signs of guilt amongst the neighbours. Why did Manus give me that odd look at Mass? Wasn't that strange, shifty behaviour from that Gallagher fella the other night at the wake? Why does Nuala's husband eye me up and down like that?

The letters created a mood of doubt and distrust within the community. But no one had the gumption to speak out. When Dinny was caught, it was a relief to all of them to be able to air their burdensome secret. None of these women pressed charges. Dinny was let off with a warning, his scandalous letter-writing career at an end.

1971. A still, spring evening. It's my last year at the tech. Soon I will be sitting for the Leaving Cert examination. In the hush I hear the rumbling roar of the distant sea, a wild throb on the horizon. It's like the loud thump of my own heart. I took a day off school to get a bit of study done but all afternoon, since the post came, I have been in a flutter of excitement. A poem of mine is included in a piece of promotional material issued by Gael Linn (the most enterprising of the Gaelic Revival outfits) to publicise Slogadh, their ambitious youth festival just then in its infancy.

When I showed it to my mother she put it to her nose and sniffed it. I told her that it was called '*Boitheach na Bó*', and was about the gush of words that came out of me the morning, many years before, when I sat by her side as she milked the cow.

'I can't read it, *a thaisce*, but I can smell it,' she said.

'What kind of smell does it have, Mammy?' I asked her, anxious to hear her olfactory critique of my poem.

'It smells like fresh milk in a bucket after milking the cow,' she said with judicious aplomb. I would have shown it first to my father but that evening he was up in the far bog paring turf banks. I had to show it to Nora John, my next-door neighbour. She's my second mother. Having no children of her own, she's taken a shine to me ever since I was a wee boy. She's a stout woman with a broad, open face and eyes that twinkle with merriment. Limpid eyes like a freshwater well. And like a well, she's a living source of stories that keep bubbling up out of her depths. She was steeping dirty socks in a basin when I walked in, a packet of Rinso washing powder at her elbow.

'It's yerself that's in it,' she said with a toothless grin. I could see the rude pink glare of her false teeth in a tumbler of water on the windowsill. They looked comical and brought a smile to my face. She only wore them now and then, to weddings and funerals, mostly. It made eating a little more ladylike on those occasions. Unlike my mother, Nora John was not of the odoriferous school of textual appraisal. When I thrust the poem under her, she peered at it attentively, one eye half shut as if trying to bring it into close focus the way I often saw her squinny an eye to study a photograph in the *Derry People*. I knew she couldn't read the poem, but this attentive and purposeful look was a way of showing her appreciation. She read out my name, 'Cathal P. Ó Searcaigh', slowly but jubilantly as if it were up in an array of lights.

'Good on ya,' she said, gripping my hand and giving it a wet, tight squeeze. Then her fluid face broke up into little rills of laughter.

'At least you have the guts to put your name to it,' she said.

'What do you mean?' I asked her.

'That Dinny fella never put a name to any of his scribbling,' she said.

'Except the dole slips,' I suggested.

'And only for that the cat would never be out of the bag,' she said, a big smile swelling across her face.

I often wondered about Dinny's letters, but those who received them either burned them or else kept them stowed away. Nobody ever showed me any of them. I asked Nora did she keep any on the off chance that she had some hidden away. She baulked at that. I could see by the way she fidgeted about on her feet and lowered her eyes that she was reluctant to talk about them.

'I just thought, maybe, you kept one or two as a keepsake,' I said jokingly.

'Some keepsake, for fecksake!' She laughed a big hearty laugh and dried her hands as if smoothing on a glove and went up to her bedroom. When she returned she held two tatty-looking letters which she handed to me.

'I was swithering whether I would give them to you or not. They're full of highfalutin filth, but now that you're a writer yerself they won't shock you.'

They floored me with their verbal high jinks and their semantic antics. Their marvellously assured wackiness amazed me. Not only had Dinny gone doolally with language, he had fabricated his own virtuoso lingo with the same mastery that made him a deft creel maker, a dazzling jeweller. This oddball local was taking language by the scruff of the neck and steering it with a loopy, daredevil recklessness towards the abyss. Compared to his bawdy headlong dash of brilliance, I realised that my own poem was tame and stodgy. It was a crushing realisation.

All afternoon, I was walking on air, uplifted by the publication of my poem. Then I'm given Dinny's letters and they deflate me with their sharp-edged ingenuity. On the day of my great literary achievement, Dinny brings me to my knees. It was ironic that my book of Greek myths which he borrowed regularly and then kept was the stimulus behind these provocative letters which were now fouling up my moment of triumph.

'What do you think?' Nora asked eagerly when she saw me folding up the letters with trembling hands. I was overcome with envy. Dinny was a true initiator of language and I was just another lousy, nondescript hack. What could I say? I stood there dumbstruck. Nora must have thought that I was reeling from Dinny's indecencies.

'Now you see what he was up to,' she said, nudging me gently on the arm. 'The cuss of a God on him but he was the devil himself with words.'

'He had a devilish way with words, alright,' I said, in a rather offhanded manner. I wanted to do exactly what Dinny had done: make words whoop and yelp with savage delight; have them violate the rules of grammar, defy the authority of syntax. Dinny's words, unlike the words in my poems, were neither bootlickers of respectability nor grovellers to correctness. They were wild tearaways; rude, lewd and crude.

'Mind you, I got a lot more but I threw them all in the fire. What the hell came over me to keep them two in the house, I don't know,' Nora said, visibly vexed with herself. I was handing them back to her but she shook her head and declined to take them.

'*Arragh*, wipe your arse with them, *a leanbh*,' and she burst out in a big pah-ha of laughing. 'Or maybe some day they'll come in handy if you want to give a bit of your tongue to somebody.'

'I'll keep them so,' I said casually and pocketed them in case she changed her mind and wanted them burned. Although I was lividly jealous at the sheer wanton genius of them and angry at how they gutted me on my day of glory, I was also sensible enough to know that they should be preserved and even wished a little that Nora had hoarded the entire oeuvre.

More than anything else I had read, these letters, in a shock of recognition, brought home to me what was vitally lacking in my own writing. Unlike Dinny, I had not yet found a voice that was uniquely my own.

Letter 1

I will nymph you. You're bullin' for a Bithynia of the Colossus. Tell that Hasdrubal of a husband of yours to give your Polyclitus a good suck. Tell him to rub his Suetonius up and down your Titus Andronicus. Get a good Agrippa of his Oracles and then pull his Pomona. When he is about to Boetus open your Pelopia and let him shag you right up to your Vitellius. I'll be at the window. I'm the bull from Crete. If you want I'll ride the fuckin' Thessalonicas out of you up in the bog. I'll Styx my Colossus of Rhodes up your tight Thisbe.

I'll take the Knossos off you if you're wearin' any and give you a good shaggin' Adrastus in the heather. I saw you going up to the altar the other Sunday and you think you have the bloody Bosporus between your legs.

Get thee to a nunnery, before I shove an asp up your dirty Tithonus. If I meet you on the road at night I'll Mount Latmus you. If you tell anybody, I'll cut your Plautus and throw your Smyrna to the dogs of Nicomedia. Kiss my Assyria you dirty Dido.

Letter 2

That husband of yours is nothing but a Heliogabalus galoot. The ugly Sisyphus of him down in Frank Jimmy's the other night talking Numidian nonsense and him thinking he's Lord Haw Haw of the bar. I had a mind to give him a good Ostrogoth in the Ptolemies but then he wouldn't be able to give you a good Giotto when he came home. That's six loads of turf he's put to the station all spadar from pissing on it to heavy it up. The gauger will be calling round some day and it won't be for tea. I hear that Scottie one is coming. Say to her that she has tits like the hanging gardens of Babylon.

That year, which was my fifth and final year at the tech, my father stopped going to Scotland. He had had enough of being away from home. He was a man who loved the solitude of open spaces and never really got used to the clamour of crammed streets or the built-up concrete sprawls that blocked his view of the horizon. 'I get lost in the terrible muddle of them blind streets,' he used to say and 'Them Glasgow streets, I'm tellin' ye, they're so hard they'd wear your heart out, never mind your bloody soles.' He was more at ease following the sheep paths of his instincts across hills and bogs of springy heather where he could see about him for miles.

When he stayed home, we survived on the dole supplemented by 'the bounty' – a sheep and cattle subsidy granted at the time to boost the livelihood of small farmers – and the odd stint of roadwork that he got. The county council had a policy of taking on local men for short spells, mostly in the winter months, to repair roads in the area.

My father was very proud of my first published poem. When I read it out to him that evening when he came home from the bog, he cried a wee bit.

'My o my,' he kept saying and gazed at me with childish wonder the way I used to look at him when I was a child, dewy-eyed and enthralled, as he chanted me a Robbie Burns poem. I knew then that the sounds he made were the strange and secret spells of a magician and I also knew that if I could match those sounds, I would have power over the adults who inhabited and controlled my world. Now my father was spellbound by the sounds I made.

I wondered did he grasp what the poem meant. It was a bit obtuse compared to the clear lyrics of a Burns poem.

'Do you understand it, Daddy?' I asked him. It sounded pompous when I said it. He fixed his unwavering blue gaze upon me.

'What kind of a witless question is that?' he said and was momentarily silenced. 'I believe in it and that's all that matters,' he said encouragingly and gave me a smile. 'It'll tell me in its own good time what it means.'

The following day, whenever he had a minute to spare, he would pick it up and murmur it to himself. The register of it was a bit bookish, cut off as it was from the living pulse of the local dialect but he stuck at it until he had it off by heart. That evening while Mammy was milking the cow, he suggested we would both go along and recite the poem in the place of its origins. We lit a candle and in that cosy, buttery glow, to the wheeze of the cows breathing and the twack of milk into the pail, I intoned my poem. My father recited it from memory. Eyes closed, he let the words out, made them rich and creamy like the milk frothing in Mammy's bucket.

When he finished, he dipped his fingers a couple of times into the milk and sprinkled a drop of it on me, my mother, the cow and even the poem. 'God bless the gift,' he said. 'May it never dry up.'

This is the poem, loose and crude and still, after all those years, endearingly bovine.

Boitheach na Bó	Cow byre
Tá boitheach na bó beo	The cow byre is alive
Lena briathra bainne	with the milk of her words
A huth chomh trom	Her udder heavy

Le foclóir	as a dictionary
A hanáil chomh tomhaiste	Her breath measured
Le dán díreach	as a *dán díreach*
Sa chuibhreann	In the field
Ólann sí a sáigh	she drinks her fill
De ghutaí gorma na spéire	of the blue vowels of the sky
Agus itheann sí a dóthain	and grazes on green syllables of
De shiollaí glasa an fhéir	grass
Lena ruball stiúrann sí	With her tail she conducts
Cor ainglí na gcuileog	an angelic choir of flies
Is lena géim mórann sí	and with her holy low
Iomann maidine an smolaigh	gives praise
	to the thrush's morning hymn
Blaisim uachtar glé	I taste her bright, creamy poetry
A cuid éigse	in my mother's bucket.
I mbuicéad mo mháthair.	

I got reasonable results in my Leaving Cert but failed miserably in maths which came as no surprise to me. Flunking maths, though, prohibited me from going to university. Mr Lally had my failed papers rechecked but not even a little leniency could up my marks because I hardly got a mark. Instead of trying to solve the problems that were posed – which were way beyond my comprehension anyway – I doodled delightfully and wrote exquisite notes about the sex lives of numerals. I wasn't too bothered. London beckoned.

I answered an advertisement in the *Irish Press* looking for an apprentice barman in a small, family-run pub in Cricklewood and within a week or two I got a positive reply. I was on my way to 'swinging London'.

Micky and Agnes were taken aback when I told them that I was heading for London – they hoped that I would stay at home and get some kind of clerical position locally – but after the initial shock they accepted it with a remarkable stoicism. No grumpy fuss, no agonising sobs, nothing that would sour my going away. Along with their fulsome blessing, they gave me three lucky charms to keep me out of harm's way. Micky gave me a wee pouch of 'Gartan clay'. This was a white powdery substance which came from the birthplace of St Colmcille and was believed to be a safeguard against death by fire and water. Agnes gave me a *'bratóg bhríde'*, an old ragged cotton scarf of hers which for years she had left out in the cow byre on St Brigid's night – 31 January – to be blessed by that matriarchal goddess on her annual visitation to herald in the spring. It was an all–round talisman that guaranteed blooming health and wellbeing. She also gave me a tiny cut of a reddish, shiny metal which was given to her by a fairy woman and was a powerful charm against the 'evil eye'. I should carry it at all times and it would counteract and undo any malignant looks levelled at me. Thus armed with their good wishes and their amulets, I went out into the world with an easy mind.

My father walked me to the bus. It was a mild morning in late November 1971. A tint of pink warmed up the hills. The smell of burning turf, a snug pungency that I would sorely miss in London, spread across the glen as people lit their morning fires. Like a cosy wrap I could almost pull it around me. At the bus stop, my father sat on a stone and smoked his pipe. Over years of going to the bus, I noticed the moss slowly creep its way over the surface of this stone with a determined patience. That morning, the tenacity of it struck me as a telling sign of what I must do to be a poet. The diligence and the patience that enabled that bit of scant moss to endure and cover the stone in a glory of green was a revealing lesson in doggedness. I needed to take heed of it.

My father had an infinitely patient approach to life and this morning, although a little tearful at my going away, he bore his grief with a calm forbearance that I appreciated. I asked him did he have any advice for me. He puffed his pipe for a while and considered the question.

'Where you're going, you'll get good advice and bad advice.' I could hear a little bird twitter in the heather to our left. 'When you know the difference between the two . . .' He paused and took a pull at his pipe. Whorls of scented smoke rose like a signal between us. 'Then you don't need any advice.'

When the bus came, he hugged me and told me to be sure and

write home once I got sorted out in London. 'And don't neglect the poetry' were his last words as I shook his hand and stepped onto the bus.

In Dublin, I had time to spare before I took the night ferry to Holyhead and I browsed the bookshops. In Webb's on the quays I read in an old musty, beautifully bound book that the Emperor Justinian (483–562) legislated against homosexuality because he was convinced that the act of sodomy was the cause of earthquakes. I didn't expect to have a sexual experience that shook the bedrock of the world, but I did hope that in London I would have one or two that at least shook the bedposts.

Kerouac made me a rucksack romantic. *On the Road* made me want to travel, to cross borders, to experience the thrill of new frontiers.

The Celts have always, I think, felt the need to journey. They voyaged in their literature into the unknown; to the isles of dreams, the isles of the ever young, the isles of fire. But they were always duty-bound to return, to share with their people the wonders they experienced, the spiritual wisdom they gained. Those things were of no consequence until they were channelled back into the community. Thus the importance of storytelling and poetry recitation.

Kerouac's rip-roaring tale of wanderlust made me want to travel, to experience the euphoria of being 'on the road'. But Nora John's wonder voyage to County Clare was equally a strong impetus to get going. Nora John never left her home, except once in her lifetime; a long epic journey to West Clare on a June day in 1963. Her sister, Maggie, was married to a Clare man and they lived in London. That year, Maggie decided to spend the holidays with her husband's relations in Lahinch, rather than with her own family in West Donegal. Nora was invited to visit them. She did but it was a flying visit. She hired a local driver, Charlie Boyle, one of the few locals to have a car at the time, to drive her there and back on the same day.

From that day onwards, her favourite topic of conversation was 'the day I went to Co. Clare'. She would describe every detail of the trip, the people that she met and the places that she saw, every twist and turn, every snatch of conversation. She remembered everything: what she had seen, heard and felt; the waitress with the lank hair and blue veins in her hands who had served her a bad egg in a café in Bundoran; the giddy chatter she had with a young policeman in Sligo when they stopped to ask for directions; the stop for a quick prayer at the Marian shrine in Knock and the fly hawkers peddling their religious knick-knacks. 'They were so fast, those buggers, they could catch your fart and bottle it.'

The damp light on the rushy fields and the closed-up houses of North Mayo saddened her. At a petrol stop somewhere near Tuam, they met a lady in a soft floral dress who invited them back to a creepy house full of cats and served them tea and iced cake. In a very privileged house near Claregalway where they stopped for a sup of water, she saw a television for the first time in her life. They took a wrong turn in Co. Clare and ended up outside a tidy thatched cottage. A biddable old man welcomed them in and played a tune for them on the fiddle after which he guided them back to the main road on his tractor.

They had tea, ham and tomatoes with Maggie in Lahinch, stayed for a couple of hours and then headed into the night back to Donegal. Driving in the dark was difficult and they strayed off course a few times but somebody would always steer them right back on the track.

On a narrow stretch of road beyond Claremorris, they veered into a ditch to avoid a speeding lorry hurtling down upon them. A drunk, wheeling a bicycle and singing at the top of his voice, staggered up to them and grinned at her, 'You're in a bit of a hole there, miss. You could do with a bit of a push,' and he laughed his head off and wandered away.

The first car that came along was driven by a young priest who took pity on them, rounded up some men and, with a push and a tow, got the car hauled out of the ditch. As they came through Barnes Mór Gap at around two o'clock in the morning, a woman in a black cape on a white horse galloped past them and filled them with dread.

'I wouldn't wish thon sight on anybody,' Nora would say and bless herself.

In the wee small hours, they eventually reached home.

When anyone told her a yarn about a trip they had taken or a journey they had made, her innocent face would light up and she'd say, 'Well, isn't that strange? That's exactly what happened to me the day I went to Co. Clare.' And that was her off on her journey of wonder once more. As the years passed, this one-day odyssey became more magical and more epic. She kept reinventing it, renewing it, marvelling anew each time at what had befallen her. Her only journey became all journeys. To quote Gary Snyder, she found a space to move in 'with her whole body, her whole mind'. She became attentive and attuned to the sights and sounds of eye and ear. She became a seer. The journey restored her, enriched, to the real world of her everyday life.

Listening to Nora John as she regaled us with her magical trip, I also wanted to travel so that I would have a tale to tell.

PART FOUR

As you set out for Ithaca,
wish that your way may be a long one,
full of adventures, full of discovery.

C.P. Cavafy

Soon, I became a dab hand at bar work and actually enjoyed doing it. The regulars were mostly Irish, men who had settled down in the neighbourhood and were raising families. They were hard-working, affable, well-to-do tradesmen who had steady jobs in the thriving building industry and came to the pub in the evening for a few quiet pints en route home.

At the weekend they brought their wives along to the pub, girls they had met at one or other of the Irish dance halls of London; the Galtymore, the Garryowen or the Hammersmith Palais. Many of the wives yearned for middle-class respectability and assimilation and touched up their homely Irish accents with a la-di-da twang to show to the genteel, half-of-bitter-sipping English that they were well bred and worthy of integration. The husbands stood by, slightly daunted by their wives' actressy posturings.

Of all our patrons, the ones who interested me most were the lonely, brooding men; labourers mostly, who lived in lousy rooms or in cheap, shabby digs. Sad, displaced men with the stench of unstoppable decay about them. Sturdy toilers of the soil, whose fathers handled stock and sowed seed on the harsh farms and starving fields of the west of Ireland. Deprived of that continuity, that community, they were social oddities in the city. The pub provided these boozers and brawlers with a little warmth, a little cheer-up matiness to fend off for a while the cold, haunted silences of their lives and to ease the daily grind of mud and mixer, transit van and trench. The pub was their club and their church, a place where they could socialise and at the same time get a little solace.

Mattie from Achill, County Mayo, was one of those men. He was a big-boned hulk of a man, a navvy. The splay of his lumpy, oversized hand on the counter when he paid with loose change was like picking a cluster of amber- and opal-coloured shellfish off some clawed deep-sea creature. He had a roundy, fair-skinned face that shone with a scoured saucepan shininess. I could hear the squish of bog in his springy step as he pushed his way through the bar-room door at around seven each night and settled down to his usual seven-pints-a-night routine and a few swigs of Powers to round it off before straggling back to his bleak room somewhere on the Edgware Road, tipsy from the reek of hopelessness.

A regular for many years, he had a proprietorial claim to a corner of the counter and woe betide anyone who took up that position while Mattie was in the bar. If one of the regulars who knew the score happened to occupy the seat, it was given up there and then when Mattie came in. The bar-room seat gave him a sense of belonging, an affirmation of his worthiness in a world that belittled him. He clung to it with unyielding attachment as if it were the linchpin of his life; a cornerstone of certainty. Sitting on that stool he was 'somebody'. It validated his life.

The bar staff upheld his right to the stool and made sure it was available to him when he came in. If, for example, a stranger dropped by in the evening and occupied Mattie's seat, the barman on duty would cleverly nudge him out of it before the big fella's imminent arrival at seven o'clock.

During one hectic shift, I was so much on the go that I neglected to notify a flashy black dude in dreadlocks to vacate the stool when Mattie entered. The Mayo man strode up the floor and scowled at this snazzy interloper who had taken his seat.

'Get off my stool.'

That beefy, six-foot-three growl silenced the bar. Mattie had a hardened dislike of blacks because, on a number of occasions when he was sloshed and out of it, he was mugged and beaten up by a gang of black thugs.

'I don't like blacks even if they're white,' he used to say. The regulars knew that there was action in the offing and ring-shaped themselves around the encounter. The manager was out and none of us fledgling barmen had the guts to intervene. A showdown was on. Mattie was gagging for revenge for past grievances.

The bully tactics didn't alarm the black man. He sipped his lager nonchalantly and ignored the threat.

'D'ye hear me? Get off my stool.'

The black bloke kept his cool and didn't budge. He just sat there and sneered at Mattie. 'Hang loose, man. There's shitloads of room here, buddy.'

'Don't fucking buddy me.'

Mattie gave him a thump on the shoulder.

'Man, don't be gettin' in my hair. Don't needle me.'

The black guy was on his feet. He grabbed a beer bottle, cracked it with a deft hand on the counter's brass trim and moved with a hoodlum swagger around Mattie, wielding the jagged edge. The overload on the fuse box of Mattie's temper was too much. His face pulsed, convulsed and sizzled. In a flash, he pounced upon his assailant, clobbering him in the balls with a mule's kick and then ramming into him with an almighty whack. The black guy groaned and slumped to the floor, clutching his groin.

'Up Mayo.'

There was a roar of approval from the Irish mob. They were proud that their own 'heavy' had trounced a brash, bottle-bold outsider. No doubt about it, I was hugely impressed too by how this hefty Mayo man could handle himself. His reaction was so wily and nifty, so crushingly fast. He was a hardened brawler, of course; a veteran of many pub punch-ups, street tussles and dance-hall scrimmages. Out of the rough and tumble of his twenty-five fracas-filled years in London, he had become a crack fighter, both feared and admired.

The black man had sagged to the floor and Mattie was grabbing him by the arse of his leather pants for another thrashing when the boss arrived on the scene.

'Mattie, are you trying to fuck up my business?'

He manhandled the Mayo man and dragged him away from his wounded prey.

'Sit down there will ya and behave yerself.'

He scolded Mattie as if he were a naughty child. Des had an authoritative presence and when he had to give some rowdy customer a talking to they took heed; otherwise, they were steered out the door and told in no uncertain terms never to return. As late as the early 1970s many of the Irish bars of North London still had a frontier viciousness about them. Des kept a good, law-abiding house because he had a rare knack of defusing any commotion before it became full-blown trouble.

'OK, boss! OK! I was just throwing a few shapes.'

In a minute he had Mattie appeased and sitting calmly on his stool. The black guy was given a slug of whiskey and recovered sufficiently to limp off to a waiting taxi. When he had gone, somebody in the pub told us that the same guy had just got out of the nick where he had served time for vicious racketeering in Willesden and Harlesden.

After that nasty clash I was more vigilant about Mattie's stool and became, in the course of things, rather fond of him. I can still hear that parched rasp of his as he ordered his first pint of the evening.

'Fill 'er up, kiddie. I've a drought the size of Donegal.'

I'd always have a word with him whenever there was a lull in the bar.

'You'll never go back now. You're here for the long haul,' he'd say, teasing me and at the same time sizing me up to see what my reaction would be to such a fate.

He himself hadn't been back for ten years. Although he earned good money, most of it got guzzled down on drink or else squandered in the betting shops. On the odd occasion when he had a stroke of luck with a horse, he would make a huge splurge in the bar and buy everyone a round or two. He spent recklessly, as if there were no tomorrow, and never saved a penny. When it came to the holidays he never had enough ready cash to take a trip back home. Anyway, he'd never go home unless he could splash out in style when he got there and impress the locals.

Christmas was the loneliest time of the year for him. Many of his mates, single men like himself, left to spend the festive season with their families back in Ireland. All work ground to a halt and he found the spare time intolerable. He was alone and abandoned in a world of merriment and family togetherness. The spangled glow of cosiness in shops and houses made him miserable.

'I can't stand all those fucking doodahs flashing at me like poxy hoors when I walk down the street.'

Christmas made him moody and sour and he took to the bottle. He'd come into the pub at midday, a haggard face, big sooty rims around his eyes, reeking of whiskey and anger. At the slightest provocation, he would yell and yelp and kick up a fuss. His rowdyness didn't ingratiate him to the wives of his fellow drinkers and he didn't get invited to their homes. At the best of times he was scruffy and crude, but more so at Christmas when he became deeply dispirited. In his glumness, he didn't make any attempt to get on the good side of any of the wives. There was nothing of the slick, smooth-talking guy about Mattie. He'd let rip and tell one of the uppity wives what he thought of her. 'You might think you're a swank, but you're talking shite from some Offaly bog hole.' These offensive remarks drove the husband into a fury, but Des would always intervene and delicately patch things up.

Christmas weighed heavily on him because it brought the grim, cheerless reality of his life into sharp focus. It showed him his failure close up. But he didn't have the drive or the self-discipline to change things. Like many of his ilk, he was set in his ways and fixed in his habits. He was, I think, fearful of change. The dreary present was more manageable than a dubious future. He was more affable when the flashy tinsel of Christmas was taken down and all that showy good cheer was put aside for another year. Then he was back to the workaday familiarity of the transit van and the trench.

He came to England in 1950, a brawny, twenty-year-old who could handle a spade and shovel with savage ease and power.

'A subbie from Belmullet gave me the start right away and I was made.'

Since then, he had laboured for countless subcontractors all over the greater London area; never anything but a hired hand, a muck-slogger and a trench-toiler. He wasn't a pushy go-getter with that sharp brashness that enabled many of his countrymen to prosper as contractors and subbies.

He was wary of officialdom and went, to a large extent, unidentified in that realm. He was distrustful of banks and didn't hold an account with any of them. Most of the time he got ready money in his pay packet, but if he got paid by cheque he cashed it in the pub. He rarely paid tax or social welfare contributions and when he did it was under an assumed name. This wilful obliteration of his identity safeguarded him, he thought, 'from them fucking snoops in authority'. In a self-imposed silence, he survived by stealth on the fringes of the system.

Sometimes he spoke with a boyish wistfulness about the Achill of his childhood; a heavily settled community of farmers and fishermen, bound together in hardship; a solidarity of the needy.

'We had a grand time of it at the mad wakes and the *meitheal*. They were great hooleys, altogether.' The *meitheal* is neighbours banding themselves together as a workforce to assist somebody with turf cutting or harvesting or potato digging or haymaking. When they finished a day's work, they often would have '*an oíche go maidin*', night until morning of merriment.

But, however fond his memories were of youthful camaraderie and togetherness in the Achill of the 1930s and 1940s, he had no illusions about the depressed state of the country. He was bitter about a system that gave him no chance to better himself.

'*Arragh*, t'was a damaged country back then with all that poverty. We had to get out or starve.' He was scathing about those who governed, all the exploitative, gombeen schemers who were permitted to flourish and hold power.

'T'was a savage country of cute hoors and conniving priests who'd snatch the holy cross off a donkey's back if they stood to gain by it. I had to get out or fucking croak.'

He was a native Irish speaker but declined to speak it. Once, when I stuck up for the language, he got quite ratty with me. 'If I was you, kiddie, I'd keep it to meself. You don't want to be a fucking Gaelic dafty in this town.'

He felt demeaned by it as if the language was some odious

deformity, a cloven hoof or a straggly tail that he had been born with and had to conceal from everyone for fear of ridicule. There was another regular, a native speaker from the Dingle Peninsula, who felt equally ashamed of the language and wouldn't utter a word of it. For him it was a down-in-the-mouth language and in his yearning for success and respectability he couldn't countenance it. Such vehement renunciation of the language by native speakers saddened me and at the same time strengthened my own resolve to uphold it. There were others who abhorred the language because of the severity of the Irish-language teachers they had in school. They were hostile to the language and hit out at it any chance they got. In their presence I kept my mouth shut. I felt sympathy for them; they had been gratuitously hurt by brutes who taught the language.

One night when the bar was quiet, Mattie told me that he had befriended a fox. Over the previous six or seven weeks he had noticed it at daybreak on his way to work lurking in a wild tangle of bushes that grew outside his room. The animal was in bad shape, feeble and scarred and unable to fend for itself.

'I took pity on him. I've a bit of fox in meself, you know, and a bit of hawk.'

He felt a strong kinship with that old, beat-up fox who had to make do like himself in a concrete jungle rather than the open countryside of his forebears. He fed him sausages and sometimes at night he'd bring him back a chicken supper from the local chipper. The fox had holed up in scrub, and came out sniffing the air inquisitively whenever Mattie approached with food. Mattie would deposit the grub at the edge of the undergrowth and withdraw to a graceful distance while the fox gobbled it up. It was a lovely dependency. The needy fox got fed and Mattie felt the better in caring for it.

'Back in Achill, I'd kill the fox. Here, I'm trying to keep it alive. It's funny the changes that can come over a man.' Eventually, that grizzled old fox died and he buried it in the brush. 'Now, I miss the poor fucker. *Arragh*, maybe I'll start looking after some lonesome bird now.' And he smiled at the dubious nature of what he'd just said. Strangely enough, that was what he did. He hitched up with an ageing hooker and moved into her house somewhere in Surrey.

On his last night in the bar, as he was leaving, he thrust a wad of crumpled notes into my hand and said, 'You're some gom but God bless you anyhow.' I shook his big lumpy hand and walked back behind the bar, tears in my eyes. When I counted the sheaf of rucked-up notes there was fifty pounds in it.

George was from Cavan but affected a posh accent, an inordinately plummy one too, which had me smiling when he spoke. He would saunter up to the counter, wiggle his index finger assertively in the air and pout his lips until he got my attention.

'A glass of fizzy orange for my Roberto. He wants something frizzante tonight and I will have my usual dry martini and don't forget the cherry; otherwise, I will have to spank you.'

I loved the lush theatrical voice and his saucy manner. Everything about George was grandiose: the over-elaborate gestures, the snooty uppishness, the wide-brimmed hats in black or sage-green velvet, the fuzzy cravats, the stagy capes. I was convinced that he was English upper crust until a gruff Cavan man who knew George's background told me bluntly, 'Don't be taking up with that poofter. He's nothing but a shite-shifter from the arse end of Cavan.'

OK! George was a fake but I admired the artifice; this put-on Englishness which gave him his distinctive hauteur; his 'deportment' as he was wont to say himself. If it was a carapace to hide his lowly Cavan upbringing, the cover-up was remarkably successful. He shaped an identity for himself, became George Smith-Jones, an English dandy, and over thirty years or more settled into it convincingly. He, unlike Mattie, opted for cohesion and became thoroughly English. It's another way of dealing with the awkward void of exile, to relinquish one's past and blend chameleon-like with the foreign mores and customs.

For some, exile is loss. You lose yourself and become another. Sometimes that can be good. The self you gain is more manageable than the self you lose. The most successful exiles, I noticed, were either those who reinvented themselves completely like George or those who had the skill to commute effortlessly between the past and the present. For many, though, exile was a land of nostalgia. They were lonely wanderers, trapped in the past.

George only came to the pub on the odd occasion. It was his local, he lived close by in Dollis Hill. He was always accompanied by the same swarthy, butch young man, and they would have a few drinks on their own and leave. I didn't get to know George well. Our only familiarity with each other was those brief exchanges of harmless banter at the counter. But he did introduce me to Matthew, a boy who would show me the variegated shadings of sex.

It happened like this. George and his moustached young muscle man appeared one balmy evening in early spring with an angel in tow. This comely youth with the lithe, slender body of a runner took my breath away. He had a smooth, oval-shaped face which dimpled beautifully when he smiled, and he smiled his sweet smile at the least provocation from George and his hirsute friend. I could not take my eyes off his tousled crop of gold-yellow hair which gleamed in the bar lights like a ripened cornfield. I wanted to gather in this golden yield and thresh it with my kisses. This shapely boy with the unaffected look was what I longed for in my fondest hopes. I had dreamed him up so many times in my solitary lust. Now he had come forth into my life, a real presence and unbidden at that. George sashayed up to the counter and ordered the drinks.

'A dry martini with your ripest cherry, a crème de menthe for my Roberto and a glass of cider for young Matthew.'

So Matthew was his name. It was a good solid name. I liked it.

Matthew! Like a mantra I kept intoning it to myself while sorting out the drinks. I kept caressing it with my tongue, slowly releasing its secret fragrance, its inner music. Matthew was both night-scented stock and a Bach canticle. Matthew! I wanted to enter the word, strip naked and run wild down its long, echoey alleys of sound. But how on earth was I going to make contact with him? I was in a sweat and a dither between holding back and making a gallant move. Would I prance up to the table and introduce myself brazenly or drop a sneaky note in his lap while collecting the empties?

They sat in their usual nook, a discreet table away from the bustle; George and Roberto taking the plush armchairs at each end of the table, Matthew reclining behind them on a couch by the wall, his beatific face edged towards the bar. I kept a close eye on them in case they upped and left without my knowing. It was a slack night and I could maintain my vigil with impunity. George and Roberto were leisurely drinkers, dainty sipsters who savoured their little tipple, but that night they were unusually hurried. They threw back their drinks and stood up as if to leave. Like a shot, I was out on the floor and heading for their table on the pretext of clearing it up.

George, with a sumptuous gesture of his hand, beckoned me to his side and proceeded to introduce me to Matthew.

'You two delectable creatures may find a little distraction in each other's company.'

He said this looking knowingly at both of us and giving Roberto a very campy nudge in the ribs.

'Roberto and I are going off to buy some *trappings* for our house. We will be back presently to collect Matthew.' He gave me a flirtatious wink and they were gone, leaving Matthew and me looking at each other timidly, unsure what to do. He stood there, stylishly understated in a long-sleeved blue sweat-shirt, white pants and trainers, waiting diffidently for me to make a move. I suggested that he come up to the counter for a chat.

He was nineteen years old and down from Norfolk to work as a bellboy in the same West End hotel where George served as banqueting manager. He was taking a year out from his studies and hoped in due course to pursue a career in the catering business. He stayed with his auntie, a childless widow in Maida Vale. The lead-in done with, we talked about this and that in an easy, natural way. He was laid back and chatty and giggled a lot, a soft puppy-like chuckle. I attended to my duties with a breezy efficiency, toing and froing with a song in my heart. No doubt about it, I was in a seventh heaven of delight. Matthew was the only customer sitting at the counter so it was easy to have an unhurried one-to-one with him.

'Are you going out with anyone?' he asked.

'No, I'm all alone. And you?'

'I'm on the shelf, too.' He smiled and I wanted to touch those pretty clefts in his cheeks; cosy nooks where you could lodge a kiss.

'You need somebody who tickles your fancy.'

I wasn't sure whether that slipped out innocently or whether he was being intentionally provocative.

'Yes, somebody you can pussy-foot around with,' I said, to see what his reaction would be.

'Somebody that stirs your stump.'

He was adept at this giddy repartee. I had never heard that expression before, but I liked the lure of it. This hot talk had me fired up.

'It's nice to be soft-soaped, sometimes,' I said, giving him a complimentary cider.

'Yeah, buttered up to your buttress.' I could see that he was keen on this oral dalliance that we were having. I sensed that it was a real turn-on for him to talk suggestively. Whatever sex I had had until then was invariably a wordless grope in the dark. I was enjoying the give and take of these exchanges. A rowdy stag party of fifteen, who were on a hectic pub crawl, dropped in and ordered a clink of drinks. It took some time before I got back to Matthew.

'It's a stiff job working in a bar,' I said, knowing that he would pick up on the implication.

'And it gets harder and harder, I'm sure, to deal with all those tipsy dicks who'd take you for a ride,' he said, with a nod of the head towards the merry stag party. By now I was so worked up that I wanted to lay hold of him and drag him off to bed. It was a hot, airless night and we were all sweating. I was so frantic that I couldn't think of anything juicy to say so I said the obvious.

'It's a steamy night.'

'It would be lovely to tuck into something cool, Charlie,' he said, taking hold of my left hand and scanning my palm as if he were a fortune-teller, his finger slowly stroking and probing my lifelines. His touch had me heedless, lacking all restraint. As I stiffened, my light beige pants had a noticeable burgeoning at the crotch. I could see him eye it keenly, the twitch and stretch of it.

'What do you see?' I said hoarsely.

He prodded the fleshy part of my palm with a moist finger.

'You're bent on having me.'

I was gobsmacked by his directness. There was nothing reticent or coy about this boy.

'Well . . .' I was caught on the hop and didn't know what to say.

'It's OK, for you I'm on tap.' And he tightened his hand around mine and giggled.

By the time George and Roberto got back we had set a date for our tryst. Monday was Matthew's day off, so I'd arrange to be off too. We would meet in the afternoon, go on a West End walkabout and spend the night at his auntie's in Maida Vale. I was astounded at the happenstance nature of all that befell me that night, the madcap way that things fell into place with a devil-may-care casualness. As they were leaving Matthew turned aside to me and whispered in my ear, 'Don't be fagged out on Monday.'

I leaned towards him, our heads almost touching, his breath hot in my face.

'I'll be bulling for it,' I said, my hand briefly nuzzling the tip of his hardened penis.

Monday was a beautiful day, the sky a bowl of Wedgwood blue, the light soft and opaline. It was the perfect day for a sultry tryst, I thought, as I sat on the upper deck of a red bus heading for the West End. We met at the statue of Eros in Piccadilly and ambled on up Shaftesbury Avenue to Soho, Matthew's hand slung casually over my shoulder. We must have looked boyishly charming to anyone who noticed us that spring afternoon, two boys in the glow of youth delighting in each other's company.

At a smart corner deli with sidewalk tables we each ordered a frothy cappuccino and a Parma ham baguette which we ate at one of the outside tables, underneath a big yellow sunshade. We sat there for a long time, sprawled out and at ease with each other, sipping good coffee and enjoying the stir and hubbub of the street. At some point a poised young woman passed by, the pert set of her breasts and buttocks accentuated by the tight lacy dress she wore. There was something mildly arousing in the wallop of her flip-flops against the hot pavement. I saw Matthew's gaze following her down the street until she turned a corner and vanished, a dreamy look in his eyes. I wondered, did he lust after women like most of the boys that I knew? Did he, too, find himself being pulled by that boundless allure?

'Is that the sort of girl that turns you on?' I said to him as casually as I could.

He looked at me as if I had said something really offensive.

'Charlie, I'm gay. I'm not one bit interested in girls.'

He was a bit nettled, I could see.

'And you? Are you or are you not?'

He stressed the 'you' in a somewhat curt manner.

I was speechless. This was the first time that somebody had asked me so explicitly whether I was gay or not. Yes! Yes! But I had never uttered that 'yes' in public although I had weighed it on my tongue for a long time, measured its heaviness, and accommodated myself to its burdensome implications. I knew that it was absolutely necessary to say this 'yes' to someone's face; a clear, unmitigated, outright 'yes', however exacting that might be. I knew that I had to break that formidable silence, shatter it with the weighty sound of a 'yes'.

Matthew faced me stubbornly and would not avert his eyes from mine. I could hear the rise and fall of his breathing, in and out in unison with my own. That was comforting.

'Yes, I am,' I said. I could hear myself say it clearly and candidly. Suddenly, it was out there, energising the ether around the two of us with its positiveness. I gazed at Matthew's beautiful face, a flawless convergence of colour and contour, and considered myself extraordinarily lucky to be coming out in such favourable company. Matthew giggled and said, 'We have to be straight up about being bent.'

He had been having sex with boys since he was fourteen, he said. At sixteen, he came out to his auntie Elizabeth in Maida Vale and later to his parents. His father was a furniture restorer and his mother a fashion writer. It was OK with them to be gay.

In the evening we walked around Soho for a while, lapping up all that sex-hustling sleaze. We were both roused by the manic hawking of excitements in those rancid twilight streets. In the window of a sex shop we noticed a pair of underpants on display, a stout prick, shaped like a pen, printed on the crotch and in bold type below the waistband this caption: 'The pen is mightier than the sword.' Matthew liked the lurid fun of that and purchased two pairs, one for each of us.

'For our nuptials,' he said, handing me the naughty briefs. 'I hope your pen is in full readiness,' and he broke into his lovely skittish giggle. We had a look at the dildos, the dick-pumps, the tit-clamps. We dipped into the magazine rack and flicked through an array of soft-porn glossies. I could see Matthew become visibly excited when I picked up a pair of handcuffs and began to toy about with them. We laughed over the life-sized inflatable dolls with names like Miss Fanny Rapture, Pussy Pandora, Jezebel Honeypot.

A tall woman, strikingly beautiful with high cheekbones and the lissom body of a dancer, showed us a very special doll with a vibrating vagina and tits that got hot. This doll, she said, was in extra thick vinyl rubber, smelled like a real woman and was called 'Pum Pum Galore'.

'You two boys could share her,' she suggested.

'We're gay,' I said, just to try out the word in public. It sounded a little timid in those sexually explicit surroundings.

'Darling,' she said and held my hand reassuringly, 'it's perfectly OK to be gay.' She must have noticed the tremble of shyness in my voice. 'Sex, be it straight or gay, dear, or anywhere in that kinky tangle in between, is just a way out of the loneliness of the self.'

She squeezed my hand and led me to a shelf with an assortment of lubricants stacked on it. 'A little fruity pleasure is what you need, darling,' she said and selected a raspberry-flavoured one and gave it to me. 'Some motion lotion to get you going.' It was a present, she said, and would not accept any payment. I was expecting a crude, hard-sell approach in a place like this and not her endearing gesture of kindness. Sally Ann was her name and we took to each other at once. She made us coffee and we lingered about in the shop for an hour or so, Matthew deeply engrossed in the hard-core bondage mags while she and I chatted. There was a steady trickle of customers and in the lulls we talked.

Sally Ann spoke grandly as if centre stage in a Wilde play and with the same aphoristic effortlessness. When I asked her was she married, she exclaimed with true Wildean sass, 'Darling, as far as marriage is concerned, I'm still in the age of dissent.' While I was there, the phone rang a couple of times and I overheard Sally Ann making arrangements to meet the different callers. One must have been a Shakespeare buff.

'How splendid,' Sally Ann trilled down the line, 'you had a midsummer's night dream about me, darling.' Pause. 'That is frightfully big, dear,' she said with bluff alarm. Pause. 'I see,' and she laughed loudly. 'It's for the taming of the shrew.' Pause. 'You want to give me the whole bang shoot,' she said breathlessly. Pause. 'Oh darling, you can have it as you like it.' Pause. 'Oh, my dear Lear, I'll come at seven. We'll do it as a two-hander.'

'You have interesting friends,' I remarked as she hung up.

'Naughty friends, I should think would be a more apt description of them,' she said and gave me a coquettish little smile. 'I take errant husbands in hand and make real for them the dreams they cannot realise in their own connubial beds.'

She pooh-poohed me when I suggested that such work must be demeaning to her.

'It benefits me, it benefits them and all in all, darling, the sex itself is much ado about nothing.'

'Let's keep in touch,' she said and gave me her number as we were leaving. As it turned out we became firm friends. Sally Ann's unabashed approach to sex was hugely edifying for me. Listening to her was far more instructive than leafing through an encyclopedia of the erotic.

After the flash-on-flash-off excitements of Soho, we browsed the more sedate second-hand bookshops of Charing Cross Road and later had dinner in a steakhouse in Piccadilly. We took the tube to Maida Vale and then walked through leafy, night-scented streets to where he lived. His aunt's house was a redbrick, ivied townhouse with big bay windows and dormers. The ground floor was spacious and elegantly laid out without any hint of clutter. A bright, ultra-modern kitchen in white and cobalt blue opened onto a large, high-ceilinged drawing room. The deep-red Turkish kilims and the vibrant, many-hued oriental rugs that were tastefully scattered over the varnished wooden floors of the drawing room set each other off beautifully and blended in an unusual mix with the dark purplish drapes and the picturesque wall hangings. The colour scheme had the oomph and dash of a Matisse composition.

Matthew told me that his auntie was a nurse. The husband, a chartered accountant with a prosperous private business, had died of cancer five years before and had left her well off and propertied. She carried on with her nursing, though, because the routine of caring for other people helped, somewhat, to alleviate the grief and pain of her bereavement. On the kitchen table we found a note which she had left for me. Her handwriting was tiny, each word delicately shaped like bird tracks across a stretch of newly fallen snow.

Charlie,

I'm on night duty and cannot meet you now but a big hearty welcome to my house. We will catch up on each other in the morning. Matthew spoke warmly of you and told me that you are an emerging poet. My late husband was an avid reader of verse and you will find a splendid collection of his books on the shelves in my bedroom. I'm so pleased for my Matthew that he has found a worthy friend here in London. Make yourself at home.

A hug and a kiss,

Elizabeth

'Matthew, will she mind us being, you know, together?' I said, fretful about the nature of our friendship. Matthew giggled and kissed me full on the mouth. 'No, not at all. She expects us to fall in love with each other, ob la di, ob la da.' Among a display of family photographs arrayed on top of a handsomely carved escritoire in the drawing room was a picture of her: a young girl in a summery dress, standing by a hedgerow. She looked so like Matthew, with the finely shaped face and that selfsame air of willowy grace that I found so beguiling in her nephew. She had been his favourite auntie ever since he was a child and now that he had come out to her those bonds were even stronger. I asked him if he knew of any other homosexuals in the family line.

'For a long time now, the gay gene has been brightening up our family bloodline like flowers along a riverbank.' He giggled and showed me a photograph of a handsome young soldier leaning on a fence post by a flowery riverbank. The young solider looked remarkably like Matthew himself. Earlier, I had noticed this picture on the marble mantelpiece in the drawing room.

'This is an old uncle of mine who fought in the Great War and never got over the death of his mate who was killed in action at the Battle of Arras in May 1917. William, according to family lore, died of a broken heart soon after being discharged at the end of the war.' He looked fondly at the photograph, put it to his lips and gave it a big smacker of a kiss.

'I have always felt a strong connection with William. Elizabeth told me recently that when I was a baby the only way to get me to stop crying was to show me a photograph of him and then I cooed blissfully. Strange.'

He showed me another photograph of a faggy middle-aged man in Bermuda shorts and a tight, poncey, lavender vest, holding a posy of pink roses.

'My uncle Bill. Elizabeth's and Dad's younger brother. He's a hairdresser in Manchester and is, as you can see, a full-time nelly.'

Matthew's room had a spare, airy spaciousness about it. A stylish, low-slung double bed with a Lincoln-green duvet was the centrepiece of the room. A framed Picasso reproduction, a Blue Period piece of a figure with a guitar, hung on the wall above the bed. A print of Monet's water lilies hung on the opposite wall. I was admiring its warm, radiant leafage when Matthew took my hand in his and remarked, 'In that work, Monet accomplished a marvellous feat. He managed to paint light in water. That's why the lily pond glows with such vibrancy.'

He had a keen eye for what was happening in the painting. That was good, I thought. With that sort of alert sensitivity I would never be bored in his company. 'Obviously, you have good responses,' I added, holding him tightly.

'I'm good at horning in on things.'

I could feel his hardness as he pressed up against me. We had bided our time with each other throughout the day, no unseemly touching, no feeling each other up. It had been an achingly sweet restraint. Now, it was time to let go.

'Let's take our clothes off,' Matthew said.

It was exciting to be in the arms of someone who reciprocated so willingly, who returned each kiss with an even more eager one. I loved that low, clear voice of his purring in my ear. It was the timbre of his voice, I suppose, a low, pulsating sound that slipped deeply into my ear cavity and gave me that delicate, indefinable pleasure. No one else has ever managed to titillate my ear in the way that Matthew did. He was a master ear-teaser.

When I put my lips to his nipple, I breathed the sweet odour of his skin, a mixture of cinnamon and musk. My hands moved down along the silky softness of his back and over the round mounds of his buttocks. When I dipped my head to his groin, which smelled of burnt almonds, and ran my tongue over the stout shaft of his cock, it was as if something within him blossomed; a little lily of desire unfurled its lovely petals of light and he seemed to glow, to become radiantly beautiful.

'You're no greenhorn at this,' he moaned in my ear, clasping me tightly and pulling me to him. Soon, we were an entanglement of limbs, a heaving swell of touch and thrust. Matthew was ravenous. He tongued me with an unsparing, all-absorbing attentiveness, his soft velvety tongue vigorous as a calf's.

'I want to tickle your fancy.'

I became a tingling nerve surge of pleasure. Outside in the night I could hear excited snatches of talk receding into silence and the feverish ebb and flow of traffic at a crossing down the street was a fit score to the warm tumult of our coupling.

During the night I woke up. Matthew was lying face downwards on the bed, fast asleep, the slatted light through the Venetian blinds making lovely, floaty shapes on his nakedness. He lay there, the dip of his back, the swell of his bum, the willow stretch of his legs, a flawless alignment of limbs, dappled in light. He was good to behold. I ran a finger over the smooth gradient of his buttocks and into the downy cleft of his arse. He gave a little childlike cry of contentment and continued to sleep. I must have nodded off too, because the next time I woke the pale rose of daybreak was brightening the bedroom. Matthew was still asleep, sprawled out on his back, the naked allure of him turning me on. We dozed off in each other's arms and only woke up when we heard Elizabeth shouting from the landing, 'Morning, boys. It's breakfast time.'

I was slightly anxious about meeting Elizabeth but as we came down the stairs the homely aroma of freshly brewed coffee coming from the kitchen heartened me. Elizabeth, in a blue muslin housecoat, was standing by her worktop whisking eggs. When she heard us enter she set aside her cooking and walked towards us with a big cheery smile on her face.

'I'm glad that England and Ireland can sometimes have a satisfying union,' she said wryly, gathering us both in her arms and kissing us lightly on the cheek. Her warm, playful welcome put me at ease immediately.

Elizabeth was in her late fifties but she had a swish youthful vigour in her movements; a bracing energy that would make anyone feel good. Tall, with wavy auburn hair which she wore in a bun, she had a trim figure and a bright, engaging face. She beckoned us to the breakfast table which she had laid beautifully with gleaming cutlery, old-time rustic pottery and white starched linen. 'It's a table fit for a queen,' Matthew quipped and we all laughed. She asked Matthew and me to read aloud a short poem of our choice from an anthology of twentieth-century verse that lay open on the table.

'My husband always read me a poem before we ate breakfast. It was our morning prayer.' I choose Wilfred Owen's 'Futility' in homage to William, the good-looking soldier who peered at us from his marble perch on the mantelpiece. Matthew read Auden's 'Lullaby'. 'In homage to all those who did have a soothing sleep last night,' he said, flashing a cute smile at me. He read it with vocal pace and mastery, bringing the poem alive with all its highbrow tenderness.

Elizabeth served a tasty breakfast of smoked salmon, scrambled eggs and coffee. We ate our food to the resonant cello strains of Bach. That was the first time that I heard a Bach cello suite and I was immediately captivated by its deep, sonorous glory.

After saying goodbye to Elizabeth, Matthew embraced me outside the door, his hand gently touching my buttocks.

'You need a surge of carnal ecstasy to get you through your hermit's week in the pub,' he whispered to me, a reference to Auden's 'Lullaby', which he had just read so touchingly.

It was a fortnight before I saw Matthew again. I pined for his presence, his touch. During those two lovesick weeks I was a slush of longing and an ache of lust. I rang the hotel where he worked a number of times but they always insisted that he wasn't available and took a message for him. Eventually, he did phone and told me, without any apparent sense of regret, that he had been busy. 'What were you doing?' I asked, in a couldn't-care-less tone. I didn't want to show him that I was upset.

'I was hanging out with George and Roberto. They were showing me the ropes.' I could hear his giddy laugh.

'When will we meet again?' I said, feigning indifference.

'Are you free tonight?'

'I can take the night off, if you like.'

'Good. Come at eight and bring your testosterone.'

It was a close, muggy night. By the time I reached Maida Vale in a hot, stale-smelling minicab, I was lathered in a sticky sweat.

Matthew opened the door to me. He had nothing on except a skimpy pair of flaming red briefs.

'I'm wearing red to taunt the bull in you,' he said, holding me by the hand and leading me down the hallway into a cool, airy drawing room. It was good to be out of the clammy night and into a fresh, invigorating space. He had the house to himself. Elizabeth had taken a break and gone off on a two-week Mediterranean cruise. In no time at all I was out of my sweaty clothes and jostling with Matthew in randy abandonment. Afterwards we lay, cuddled around each other on a shag-pile rug on the floor, and slumbered. When we woke up, I had an urgent need to go to the toilet and crap. Matthew sensed this and asked unabashedly, 'Can I watch you while you're doing a poo?'

I was horrified at the request. 'Definitely not! I'd be too ashamed to let you see me.'

'Why?'

'For God's sake, it's such an intimate act. You don't want to sniff my poop, do you?'

'Yes, I do. I want you to dip my nose in it.'

'Why do you want to demean yourself like that?'

'I'm not going into any cheap psychobabble about the why of it all. Ever since I remember, excrement has excited me.'

I shuddered at the idea of Matthew watching me. Most of the time I was too ashamed to defecate in a public lavatory in case someone in the next cubicle overheard the plop of my turd in the bowl or, even more humiliating, in case someone was peeping at me with my trousers down. I found the stench of my shite offensive and always carried cheap spray to remove the whiff of it, especially if invited to someone else's house. I couldn't reconcile myself to this most human of functions. At home, Micky and Agnes relieved themselves with uninhibited ease in front of me. Often at night, one or other of them got up and defecated loudly in the latrine bucket which we always kept in our bedroom. Unlike them, I had a real dread of being seen evacuating my bowels.

'Matthew, I'm really sorry that I can't oblige you but I have a big hang-up about all this stuff,' I said, pleading with him.

'You're just a snarled-up prude!'

I could feel the contempt in his voice.

I rushed down the hallway, locked myself in the toilet and turned the wash basin tap to full flow so that he couldn't hear me shitting. When I returned, he was sitting cross-legged on the settee, staring sullenly into space and wouldn't respond to anything I said. I dressed and was about to leave when the doorbell rang. Matthew hopped off his seat and moved towards the door, stark naked.

That was odd. He must know, I thought, who's at the door. I could hear the door opening, a burst of laughter and Matthew saying, 'Please don't ring the bell. It's much more fun to pull the doorknob.'

And then the click–clack of footsteps down the hallway and Roberto appeared in the drawing room wearing a long, black leather overcoat and spurred cowboy boots. He was holding a bulging plastic carrier bag that was ripping up. When he set it down on the settee it tipped over and some of the contents slopped out: a riding whip, a pair of handcuffs, some tethers.

Matthew saw me eyeing the tackle.

'You will have lashings of fun, wait 'til you see,' he said to me in a coaxing voice. He was fired up by the torture kit.

'I think a trio will strike a chord with you.'

He slunk up to me, threw his arms around my neck and flashed an ingratiating smile. He was trying his best to wheedle me into having a whip–up with them. I had no interest whatsoever in a brutal debauch with Roberto and him. The idea of it sickened me. As well as that, I was annoyed with Matthew. I didn't like the sneaky underhand way he had brought Roberto on the scene. It was a set-up. He had deceived me and I was upset by that. I brushed him aside and stood apart from them. Roberto didn't speak a word. He looked brutish and ugly. Slowly and deliberately, he took off his coat, glaring at Matthew and myself with a fiendish gleam in his eyes. Underneath the coat, he didn't have a stitch on. His body, bristly with thick, thorn-like black hair and hung with a big, gruesome penis, gave me the creeps. In the raw, he looked like a heinous demon out of hell. He frightened me. I sidled away from him, out towards the door leading into the hallway. I wanted to get out of there before he clapped me in irons. In brute strength, I knew that I was no match for him. When he began to rummage in his torn bag of equipage, I fled down the hallway and out the front door in double quick time. I could hear Matthew yelling after me, 'Charlie, it's not cricket, leaving like this.'

Out on the street with my heart thumping furiously, I nearly fainted but managed to hold on to a lamppost until my fear subsided. Once I got a little strength back I hailed a minicab and taxied home.

'What's the matter, son?' the driver said, in a very soothing Cockney accent when he heard me sobbing in the back seat.

'My girlfriend has just gone off with a very violent Italian gigolo,' I blurted out.

'Take no notice of it, son. Girls will come and girls will go until the right one steps for good into your heart.'

That made me smile.

After that night, I never laid eyes on Matthew again. I didn't make any attempt to contact him and he didn't seek me out, either. Much as I liked his angelic good looks, his racy humour, the zest he had for living, I was ill at ease with the more daring aspects of his sexuality. There, we were mismatched. The accelerated tempo at which things had happened didn't help either. I like to modify my ways slowly, to amend and adapt gradually. He pushed me to the limits, too soon. There were nights when I hungered for his sweet touch, but somewhere in the course of those hot imaginings he would always turn to me and say something crass, like 'Let's go to the loo and do a whoopsie together', and that, alas, doused my passion.

Shortly after my parting with Matthew, I had an experience which, in no small way, helped to ease the defecation anxieties. It was my day off and I was wandering around Mayfair when I came across a small innovative gallery, somewhere off Grosvenor Square, with a show that caught my attention. Ordinary objects were transfigured by being placed in unusual juxtapositions. I remember a stiletto shoe placed beside a child's drawing of a cat. The cat gave the impression of a slinky stiletto and the shoe seemed to have taken on a wily, feline appearance. It was titled 'Pussy-footing'.

The one, though, that stands out in my memory is a green toilet bowl with a turd and a red rose stuck in it. I was intrigued by what I thought to be at first an inappropriate association, but gradually it struck me that the turd and the red rose were not at all at odds with each other. In fact, they complemented one another. They were both signs of aliveness. Normally I would frown at the turd and admire the rose. This artwork was a joyous salute to flowers and to faeces alike. It was asking me to accept these two elements on an equal basis. I was so ashamed of shitting that I had detached myself from the actuality of it, disengaged myself from it as if it weren't happening to me. I couldn't bear its messy humanness. Looking at this exhibit, I was, somehow, made to see that shitting was a wholesome function, as naturally beautiful as a flower, and that I had to acknowledge it and integrate it into my life. That was, for me, a huge breakthrough, a bowel-moving epiphany, you could say. I didn't run out onto the street singing the praises of shite or rhapsodise over it at Speaker's Corner, but I did develop a healthier, more natural response to this function from then on. In fact, that day I plucked up the courage to go to the loo in the gallery; a small privy which wasn't really very private as it was wedged between the exhibition space and an administrative area and I pooed with only a smidgen of shame.

One night I chanced upon a nice boy at a cinema in Trafalgar Square. He was on his own and standing ahead of me in the small queue; a clean-cut, strong young man. Now and then, he turned his head and eyed me up and down. I let on to be ignorant of his attentions but I was, of course, getting a real buzz out of being pursued. He purchased his ticket and then held back, lingering in the foyer while I bought mine. He was a well-built boy with a lean, pleasant face, his thick black hair combed back from a high, curved forehead and parted in the middle. It glistened with hair oil, which under the foyer lights gave his head a lovely glow. His face had nothing of the divine beauty of Matthew's. His was a more ordinary, boy-next-door face with just one strong distinguishing feature: his fleshy, sensuous lips.

When I headed for the auditorium, he followed me into the same row and sat down a seat away from me. I have no clear memory of the main feature other than a dizzy plot involving gypsy intrigue, drug trafficking and furious car chases on heady, hairpin bends.

I was too gripped by the pressing drama at hand to pay too much attention to the film. I could see that my pursuer was getting restless from the way that he shuffled about uneasily in his seat. Now and then he gripped his armrests as if about to make a sudden shift but he always floundered and sank back with a suppressed groan. I knew that he was aching for contact, but I wondered would he ever become bold enough to make a move. The empty seat lay between us like a chasm. If he didn't make haste I would have to take the initiative myself. More than halfway through the film he was still anguishing, but a kiss on the screen must have emboldened him – 'stiffened his resolve', Matthew would have said – and he was up all of a sudden and into the vacant seat beside me. Lucky for us there weren't many patrons in the cinema. We were alone in the back and could indulge ourselves to the full. Soon we were stirred up in a pleasurable fumble of roaming hands and a happy disarray of clothes and edging slowly and inexorably to a lovely vertiginous moment of bliss.

As the credits were rolling, I made for the toilet. He followed hot on my heels and stood right beside me at the urinal watching me pee. At the time, we were the only ones in the toilet.

'My name is Hugh. What's yours?'

He had a thick, throaty English accent but there was something else there, a lilt, which mellowed it slightly.

'I'm Charlie.'

'It's good to meet you. You're Irish.'

'Yes!'

'I'm London born but of Irish parents, too. We live in Finsbury Park.'

That was what I'd heard, an Irish swing to his more sober English accent.

'Which part of Ireland do they come from?' I asked, washing my hands. I could see him in the mirror. He was watching me.

'They both come from the Letterkenny area of County Donegal. Are you familiar with that part of Ireland?'

That stunned me. I wanted a fling with someone who knew nothing of where I came from. This was too close to the bone. What if he was visiting his folks in Letterkenny and talked about me? An inadvertent slip of the tongue and the word would be out about my queerness. I didn't have the strength of character to contend with that disclosure yet. I wanted to keep the lid on my secret until an opportune moment came and then I would reveal it myself. I was being unreasonable, of course, but fear makes us anxious and, indeed, over-suspicious.

'Actually, I'm from the south of Ireland. I have to go now to visit an auntie who is on her death bed in Lambeth,' I said to him rather brusquely.

He was gutted. I could see that from the forlorn look on his face. A rush of people came into the toilet and we moved out.

'I want to meet you again, Charlie.'

He was making a desperate plea. I knew it from the choked-up way that he spoke. I gave him a false number, told him that I was working on a building site in Wimbledon and assured him that we would meet within a week.

'Maybe we can go on a weekend trip together if you're free, sometime,' he said to me as we were parting outside the cinema.

'That would be nice,' I said, noncommittally.

We parted with a handshake and a promise to meet soon. As I walked down Whitehall to Westminster Bridge to clear my head, I cringed in shame at the deplorable way that I had deceived this lovely boy.

Now and then George and Roberto came to the pub for their usual dainty tipple, sometimes a martini and a cherry brandy, or a pink gin, maybe, and a snowball. Unlike most of our trade, they certainly weren't stuck in the rut of the pint. George always bought the drinks as Roberto lounged in the corner. He seemed less of a threat now than he was that night at Matthew's when I found him so menacing. Nevertheless, there was an edginess about him that made me tense, a strained wild-cat bent of the body as if he were about to pounce. I kept my distance. I assumed George knew about my romp with Matthew but he never alluded to it. When he wished to be judicious, George had tact and prudent good manners.

The last time I saw him, he was on his own. Roberto had gone off to Rome to visit his family. He ordered a large vermouth with the customary cherry, sat at the counter, spread out a pale ivory-coloured hanky on his knees and with a file and cutters proceeded to manicure his nails with regal aplomb, taking the occasional coquettish sip from his glass. His cheeky effervescence and his unmanly behaviour was a challenge to some of our more intolerant patrons, particularly the Irish wives who scorned him, but on the whole the men were amused by George's laughable affectations.

At the time I was caretaker-manager of the pub for just a couple of days, while the boss took a short break. George, when he was leaving, patted me on the back for running the place so efficiently.

'Sometimes it's good to get a crack of the whip,' he added, and winked mischievously at me.

'George, I'm not interested in whips,' I told him rather sternly. I was still a bit touchy over the set-up at Matthew's. George looked at me anxiously, took my hand in his and stroked it gently.

'My dear boy, you don't know what you're missing, and

besides, don't ever exclude anything from your agenda of pleasure.'

He kissed me, a big puffy peck on the cheek, and went out into the night.

'He's got this barmy notion into his head that I'm going to marry him,' Sally Ann told me with unruffled poise as she swept down the stairs in a frothy red dress like a cascade of bougainvillea.

'It would cost him an arm and a leg, of course, to be hitched to *moi*,' she said and stepped nimbly off the stairs into the sitting room. 'And a whole lot more on enhancing his rather piddling member.'

A gurgling sound deep in her throat bubbled up into laughter.

'Size is not important, but there's a difference, darling, between undersized and stunted.' She waved a photograph of him in front of me; a portly man in a herringbone suit, a stiff collar and cuff links. He was one of her clients, a middle-aged lawyer who came to her twice a week for what she called 'delicate cardiovascular manoeuvres'.

'You're not going to marry him,' I said disapprovingly.

'You sound like a Vatican edict, dear,' she purred and stroked my arm. Her gold chain jingled with expensive charms. 'I want to manipulate a man, but I don't want to marry him.' Touching up her lips with a stick of cherry-red gloss, she twitched her mouth into an oddity of shapes.

'What I really need is a well-endowed sugar daddy.'

A book of nursery rhymes lay open on the floor at 'Hickory Dickory Dock'.

'Mr Dobbs, the lawyer,' she explained, 'has an infantile craving for games involving nursery rhymes.' The latest, she told me, required her to dress as a nanny, sit at one end of the sitting room while he, heavily nappied, sat at the other end. They rolled a soft ball along the parquet floor, back and forth to each other, keeping the flow going by reciting, slowly and suggestively, some nursery rhyme or other, gradually building up the tempo of it, passing the ball to and fro faster and faster and spitting out the words with wanton abandon.

'Twenty minutes of that naughtiness and he's spewing like an active volcano.'

What I liked about Sally Ann was her calm acceptance of the whole gamut of human sexuality; that chunky catalogue of quirks and caprices and seething desires. Her broad-minded tolerance was as beautifully faceted as the lustrous sapphire swinging from her neck.

'Drinkies, darling,' she drawled and motioned me to a mirrored sideboard well stocked with bottles. She poured two glasses of red wine, handed me one and glided to a rocking chair in the middle of the floor. Slowly, she tilted back and forth, holding her long-stemmed glass as lightly as if it were a fragile red lily. The room glowed with a low peachy light which came from three fancy porcelain lamps, draped with pale silk scarves, arranged cleverly around the place.

A photograph on the wall above the sideboard caught my eye. It was Sally Ann as a young girl, long legs and ribboned hair, wearing a green pinafore, standing in front of a fairground carousel.

'Lovely photo,' I remarked.

'That's me, darling; an off-duty waif escaped from a Dickens novel.' She looked at it thoughtfully.

'In that folksy outfit I used to fool around with the manager of the funfair, a very naughty man. He loved dressing me up in Victorian garb.'

She sipped her wine with a cool, elegant nonchalance as if what happened was perfectly normal. 'Naughty' was Sally Ann's severest rebuke for any kind of sexual deviancy.

It was my first visit to her place, a posh address in Kensington. 'A neighbourhood of topcoats and well-kept pets' was how she described the area as she showed me around the flat on my arrival: two luxurious ensuite bedrooms upstairs with mounds of opulent muslin swathed across the balconied windows; a kitchen; a sitting room and a bathroom on the first floor; all rigged out with the appurtenances of the well-off.

'Very stylish,' I told her, gobsmacked by the sheer plush of it. She lowered her eyes in feigned modesty.

'I live in style, darling and I do hope I'll die in style.' She got a slim glass vase and with a deft touch adorned it with a posy of freesia I had brought. 'With a little bit of luck, style will be the last of my senses to go,' she said and placed her pretty display on a marble-topped coffee table in the sitting room.

Since I had met her in the sex shop, Sally Ann had taken me in hand and shown me the sights. On slow strolls around the seedier side of London, she took me to tucked-away gay venues, to hoodlum hangouts, to alleyway strip clubs.

'Darling, I'm a boulevardier of the carnal,' she told me on one of our walks and flashed me a wicked smile.

'Do you ever worry about the morality of all this sleazy sex business?' I asked her. She pursed her lips and gave me a scowling look, as if I had said something terribly indecorous.

'I have no morals, darling, but a lot of compassion,' she vented at me. Sally Ann had adorable class; a haze of alluring perfume hung in the air as she walked. She carried herself with the gamine chic of the catwalk. There was a zing to her swinging step that made men stare at her with lust in their eyes.

A month before, she had introduced me to an olive-skinned youth of Indian parentage, a lovely boy, lamb-like in his demeanour. She knew his people, a moneyed Delhi family in the fabric business. Devendra was eighteen years old and on a short visit to his relatives in North London. On our first outing walking on Hampstead Heath in companionable closeness, I let my hand linger gently on his backside and noticed the excited tensing of his buttocks. Very soon we veered off the track for a twilight tryst in a grove of shady bushes.

Over the three weeks that he stayed in London, we met as often as we could; ours was an easy confluence of cultures. I took him to an Irish pub and he took me to an Indian restaurant. He spoke English with a comic Hindi quaintness that beguiled me. And he exhibited a view of the world that was not unlike my mother's in that he believed in signs and portents.

On the eve of his departure, we booked into a shabby hotel near Euston Station and rolled about on a lumpy mattress with a wild, turned-on urgency as a thunderstorm lit up the London night. As a parting gift, he gave me his favourite book. It was *Gitanjali* by Rabindranath Tagore.

Sally Ann did not talk about her past. Once when I broached the subject, she dismissed it with a laugh. 'Darling, my past is veiled in seven deadly enigmas. A girl like me you should realise only has a present.' She ran the Soho shop with great success. Most likely she had a stake in the business and it gave her the added incentive to make it gainful. And then she had her set of well-off gentlemen who paid her handsomely for being 'their erotic domestic'.

Now, she sways back and forth in her rocking chair and takes dainty sips of wine while I comb her long, very fine reddish-blonde hair with an ivory-handled brush. It's a mild Sunday evening in November and we can hear church chimings as she tells me about her clients. Like Mr Dobbs, most of them have specific needs. One has to be slapped severely on his bare bum and then hauled screaming, like a child, to a potty where he's ordered to poo at once. Another requires her to be starkers except for her earstuds and a smile, and play Ludo with him. A property tycoon has a penchant for dressing up as Marie Antoinette and Sally Ann is his bossy lady-in-waiting who spanks him for any unqueenly behaviour which over three hours amounts to many petty infringements of decorum and so a steady walloping of buttocks.

This particular evening she is dressed in her low-bosomed, slit-at-the-legs red dress to accommodate a special client, an oil-rich sheikh, her 'prince of Arabia' she calls him, who loves her in red. She is going to 'have dessert with him', at his suite of rooms in a Park Lane hotel, which entails him eating a helping of cherries, cooked in cream, out of her vagina.

'I'm frightfully tattle-tale, darling,' she says and flutters her eyes in coy innocence. She glances at her jewelled watch. 'Holy smoke, I'm going to be late for dessert.' She puts on a pair of black lace-up velvet shoes, throws a chiffon scarf across her shoulders and off we go to hail a taxi.

'Misbehave yourself, darling,' she calls and blows me a big kiss as the taxi speeds her off into the night.

Soon after that, I received a postcard from Sally Ann enclosed in an envelope. She was holidaying in Greece.

Charlie, I'm having a wonderful time here in Athens. I love the old ruins. In fact I had dinner with a dear old ruin last night, a New Yorker with plenty of boodle. Hard cash is much more desirable, darling, than a hard dick. He wants to take me on a tour of his ancient sites. As you know, Charlie, I'm more interested in histrionics than history. I'm not sure whether he said 'I will take you to the Acropolis' or 'I will take you on the Acropolis'. His wife, Esteme is her name, has gone to Lesbos with her girlfriend. Queer, isn't it? He is a rich old sod and is crazy about me, I think. He calls me Pandora. Only hot lolly I told him opens my box of tricks. Pray, Charlie, that my rapacious desires are entirely answered. Social survival, darling, is rather crass, isn't it? I hope you are being pricked into poetry on a regular basis.

Lots of Greek love,

Your Sally Ann Pandora

I hardly ever went to any of the pubs or the dance halls where the Irish socialised in London. The areas of Cricklewood, Kilburn and Camden Town were sprawling overseas parishes of Ireland and in many ways as insular and tribal as any rural Irish community. I found their localist outlook stifling and didn't engage with it at all. I went elsewhere. The West End was a thrilling stomping ground for an eager youth. I spent most of my free time there: a West End *flâneur*, if that word can be appropriated for strolling in any city other than Paris.

I'd walk around those streets, awed by their imperial sweep and their architectural grandeur. The oomph may have gone out of the swing and the colour may have faded from the costumes, but for me, it was still 'swinging London'. Carnaby Street, once the in place for counterculture costuming, was just a big dowdy clothes rack but, however old, I loved its exotic tatter. Marc Bolan with his iconic hair and ambiguous get-up was the teenage idol of style and glamour. That spring, that summer of 1972, he was everywhere. His face beckoned from billboards, his records blared from music shops. In clubs, I caroused to 'Metal Guru' and, one humid dawn, I made love to a young American in a house in Bayswater while somebody in the next room played 'Get It On' over and over. He laughed his head off when I suggested to him that he had a T-erextion.

'I sure have,' he said, 'and I'm horny enough to Ride a White Swan.'

That summer, going to cafés, hanging out with Sally Ann, enjoying one-night encounters, the buzz of Marc Bolan thrilled the airwaves of my senses. I was tripping on what B.P. Fallon famously called 'T-recstasy'.

Charing Cross Road with its treasure trove of bookshops was my favourite place. It was there that I began to familiarise myself in earnest with modern poetry from around the world. The Penguin Modern European Poets series was an incalculable asset to those interested in what was happening in poetry throughout Europe.

The scathing tact and the dazzling shifts of subterfuge practised by the East European poets of the 1960s left me gasping with admiration. Under the hydra-headed monster of totalitarianism with its creepy censorship, Zbignew Herbert in Poland, Miroslav Holub in Czechoslovakia, Vasko Popa in Yugoslavia, Marin Sorescu in Romania all became connoisseurs of cogent irony, virtuosos of outspoken obliquities and well-versed masters of poetic double-talk. With an impulse towards the parable rather than the polemic, they astounded me with the tightrope artistry of their poetry.

I became acquainted with the poetry of Yevtushenko, Neruda, Saba, Tranströmer, Pessoa, Montale, Lorca, to name just a few of the poets I read but I fell head over heels in love with the poems of Constantine Cavafy (1863–1933).

I found him in the ebullient, all-embracing poetry section in Foyle's. I was reaching for Causley and somehow dislodged Cavafy and he came tumbling down at my feet. Until then, I was unaware of him. I picked him up and began to read. It was love at first sight. I bought a book and retired to a nearby café. It was *The Complete Poems of C.P. Cavafy* translated by Rae Dalven. I was enthralled by the poems, by their quiet, ironic, self-deprecating speech as they talked with a total lack of sentimentality about the evanescence of life and love. I loved, of course, the frankly homosexual poems, his own autobiographical erotica set in Alexandria. The direct way he had of evoking an erotic event or a sensual emotion with electrifying drama made a lasting impression on me. The no-linguistic-frills but plenty-of-erotic-thrills mode of poem that he wrote about his youthful pick-ups excited me physically and imaginatively. I was having my own 'first, fine, careless raptures', artistically speaking, and indeed my first, fine, careless ruptures, anally speaking, with Matthew and others. These poems of Cavafy's intensified both experiences. Poems in which past pleasures, the intoxicating pleasures of the flesh, are remembered so fiercely, so keenly that they come alive again with a throbbing immediacy. By means of memory, the fleeting erotic encounters of his youth, the passionate short-lived affairs in the seedy neighbourhoods of Alexandria, are recreated so that they achieve permanence through the transforming power of his poetry, the timelessness of his art.

This Cavafian notion of memory – the redemptive power of memory to hold and to transform into art the ephemeral passing life of the senses – appealed to me enormously. In Greek mythology, Mnemosyne is the spirit of remembering. The Greeks held her to be the foremost muse. Memory is a brilliant faculty. It's the stuff of genius really – having the capacity to explore our buried self; the shards of this and that – joy, sorrow, grief, happiness, loneliness. We have many lost worlds buried deep in the earth of our psyche, a whole Atlantis of feeling. Nothing is ever forgotten by the body. Memory is the means to dig, to unearth, to discover the ages of our being, the artefacts of our feelings.

Many of his poems are miniature dramas presented with a detached irony, set in a remote historical past somewhere between

200 BC and AD 600 – his favourite age being the Panhellenic world of the diasporic Greeks in Europe and Asia Minor after the collapse of the Alexandrian Empire. I was intrigued by his resourceful use of an assemblage of characters from the ancient world – an imaginative masking device that allowed him to distance himself from his own contemporary angst, and at the same time enabled his poems to become universal statements.

In the following weeks, I read and reread the poems and at the same time mused over my own brief sensual encounters. I began to write poems that were, I felt, infused with the spirit of Cavafy. His sense of place enthralled me. I marvelled at the way he brought those locations alive, far-flung places, for me then, of romance and mystery, charm and colour; places like Alexandria and Antioch; Beirut, Cappadocia and Constantinople; Ithaca and Ionia; Lebanon and Nicomedia, Sidon, Syracuse and Syria.

Late one night in my small room above the bar – a room that had bright russet wallpaper which always reminded me of the reddish glory of autumn-coloured bogs at home – it struck me that I should give Mín A Leá and its environs a literary aura, a kind of Cavafian charm, so that Caiseal na gCorr, for instance, would become as erotically charged as Alexandria in the gay imagination. As it happens, Caiseal na gCorr – the fort of the cranes – can also be construed as 'ancient stone fort of the queer'. For those in the know, this etymologically bent reading would give it a playful, homoerotic subtext. Close to Caiseal na gCorr, there's another townland called Baile an Geafta, meaning the 'townland of the gate', but mysteriously rendered into English as

'Gaytown'. Cavafy would, I know, appreciate that creative corruption. As I pondered this, I began to recite a litany of townlands; Mín A Leá, Mín na Craoibhe, An Dúnan, Mín na bPoll, An Mhín Bhuí, Fana Bhuí, Caiseal na gCorr, Prochlais, An Bhealtaine. These were the hill settlements of *home* where the wild peaty moors had been domesticated into neat fields and orderly farms.

Home! The word heaved its way up from somewhere deep within me. Then a terrible bout of homesickness overcame me and I began to sob out the names of places on our farm in Mín A Leá, names which I committed to memory when I was a child out walking the fields with my granda: Sruthán an tSiolastraigh (the wild iris stream); Seascann an Bhachráin (the swamp of the bogbean); Ard na gCearc Fraoch (the hillock of the grouse); An Casan Glas (the green path); Páirc na hAbhna (the river field); Garradh Beag na nÚll (the wee garden of the apples); Bachtaí na Locha (the turf banks by the lake); Áithe an Bhealaigh Mhóir (the limekiln by the road); Casan na Láchan (the duck path); Féarach na Bó (the cow meadow); Ard na gCloch Gorm (the hillock of blue stones). The more I named our farm, the more I pined to be back there with Micky and Agnes. It was that, a wistful longing for a patch of earth, but it was something else too, an ache to be rooted in the *dúchas*.

Dúchas is a difficult word to explain in English, but briefly it means a sense of connection; a feeling of attachment to a place, a tongue and a tradition; a belief that one belongs to a sustaining cultural and communal energy; that one has a place and a name. I had to return home to reclaim my heritage, my *dúchas*. And *dúchas*, I was telling myself, was not going to be a flight into the past. It was going to be a quest rather for an expanded present which would flow backwards and forwards with one and the same movement.

Home! The word was a discovery – but what is discovery, only what we remove the cover from? It has always been there – only hidden. I also realised that Irish was my emotional language, and not English. Intuitively, I knew more about the texture and the tone, the aura of words in Irish. The language inhabited my consciousness in a way that English didn't. That was what was wrong with the poems that I was writing in English, they were in psychic exile from my mother tongue. From then on I was determined that I would write poetry only in Irish.

I knew that the language linked me to a wellspring of tribal memories; an archive of ancestral experiences, a library of folk wisdom that was distinctly Gaelic. I felt that I belonged to something peculiarly enriching; something with its own irreplaceable value system. I would be able to assert myself and withstand being absorbed and assimilated into whatever standard was being foisted on me from elsewhere.

The Irish language would, I believed, enable me to be uniquely myself, to have a distinctively native viewpoint, my own radiant window of wonder onto the world. Strangely enough it was Cavafy, a writer who loathes sentimentality, who triggered in me this keen lonesomeness for home. For me it was an intensely revelatory moment and it strengthened me. I knew for sure that it was only in Gaelic that I could lyricise my experiences and within the artifice of a poem make them whole and permanent. At the time I recalled a Hans Christian Andersen story that I had read years before. It was in a book that my father picked up from a bargain pile at the Barrows – Glasgow's famous flea market – and concerned a shadow that longed desperately to become a man. Until then I was that shadow, lost and insubstantial, trailing between two languages. Now, with my newly revealed sense of purpose, I became real.

A man able to voice himself, confidently, I hoped, through his chosen language.

That night I read through what poems I had written in English in the six months I had been in London and decided that they were worthless. The dynamics of my own experience were not getting into a language that was credible. None of them had the individual pitch of an original poem. In a moment of unsentimental desperation, I tore them up into tiny fragments and dumped them in the rubbish bin downstairs. It was a necessary purging and I felt relieved as if I had got rid of my sins in the confessional and walked out, freed and unburdened, with a cleansed conscience. I was now ready, as it were, to live in the state of grace that was Gaelic.

I kept one though, not so much for its literary merits but in memory of Devendra. The poem was heavily indebted to the self-consciously visionary musings of Tagore and especially derivative of the *Gitanjali* book Devendra had given me. 'Sometimes on a Night of Unfathomable Darkness a God Appears' was the rather pedantic title of it.

> Beloved, you came from the night.
> You entered my darkened room, the secret
> room at the core of my being; you lit it
> with the lamps of your gleaming eyes.
> You sat me at the glowing hearth
> of your affection; you touched me
> with the sweet song of your kindness.
> You caressed my human heart
> with your gentle smile.
> You bathed my weary limbs
> in the warm divine waters
> of your love. My young god of life,

of lust, you filled my cup of solitude
with the red wine of passion.
That night, my angel of light, you stirred me
with life and with death.

I returned home in early September 1972. That night the crossing from Holyhead to Dun Laoghaire was very choppy. I sat opposite a short, stoutish elderly priest with a country face who reminded me of Granda. Whenever the ship swayed in a heavy swell he looked up, slightly alarmed, from the Barbara Cartland romance he was reading and blessed himself. Occasionally, he'd put the book aside and extract a round silver snuff-box from his breast pocket. He had small, dainty, fluttering hands. Delicately, he'd dip a thumb and forefinger in the powder, take a pinch and raise it ceremoniously to his nostrils. A very precise, measured snort, at first in the right nostril and then in the left one and repeated until the transmutation of snuff into pleasure was completed. He'd shut his eyes momentarily and a gentle childlike gratification spread across his ageing face and then he was back to his book, livened up a little, the better to savour Miss Cartland's juicy amours. The gingery piquancy of his snuff brought me back to my very early childhood when most of the elderly women in the area were compulsive snuff-takers. 'Sure a wee pinch of snuff lights up yer head and, God forgive me, lets ye into heaven by the back door,' was how one obsessive snorter described the allure of it.

To pass the time, I took out *Dineen's Dictionary*. A few weeks before, I had come across it in a basement charity shop in Camden Town. It had a beautifully penned inscription, '*Do Mháire ó Eoghan, Caísc 1966. Go neireochaidh an saol linn aimsear seo na haiséirí'* – 'To Mary from Owen, Easter 1966. May we prosper in this season of the Resurrection.' It's much more elaborate than that in the original, more multi-faceted in its meanings than my limp translation suggests. For a start, *'aiséirí'* means both resurrection and resurgence and *'Go neireochaidh an saol linn'* implies literally that the world may rise up with us. *'Aimsear'* alludes to both weather and the passage of time. Easter 1966 was of course the fiftieth anniversary of the 1916 uprising. The book was in mint condition and I wondered did Máire, whoever she was, even open it. How it ended up in a pile of grubby, dog-eared thrillers in a charity shop, I will never know. The vagaries of fate, I suppose. The inscription gave it a certain character that a newly bought book off the shelf would not have. I bought it for a pittance, the sales girl having no idea of its value.

Dineen's Dictionary, a lively, idiosyncratic word hoard, is a truly fascinating insight into the world, the psyche of Gaelic. It could be described and I misquote Eliot, as 'notes towards the definition of the Gaelic world-view'. I was becoming more heedful of the fact that Gaelic was my chosen literary filter through which I saw the world. A skim through *Dineeen's* allowed me to increase my word power and also to chance upon extraordinary gems of lexical wit.

Seeing the priest, I recalled the definition of *'sagairtín'*, 'a little priest, an inedible periwinkle and a ram with one testicle missing'. Like any wary countryman in a strange place, the priest kept a close eye on the bag at his feet, a bright-green holdall which caught my attention. I leafed through *Dineen's* until I found *'glas'*. The adjective *'glas'* – green – has an assortment of shadings in Gaelic. *'Glas'* is green in vegetation but if it is used to describe a horse, the animal is grey. *'A maidin ghlas'* for example doesn't mean a green morning but a raw, chilly one. If someone has a '*súil ghlas*', you are describing an eye colour that hovers somewhere between light blue and grey. '*Glas*' in cloth usually means a grey, undyed homespun material. '*Glas*' can also mean a bolt or a lock, a wee stream or an unaccustomed hand at doing something. There are forty shades of '*glas*'.

At some point, I put *Dineen's* aside and ventured up on the deck to get a breath of air. I was standing alone in an unlit corner, taking in the salty night breeze, when a boy in old-fashioned clothes who smelled of carbolic soap stood right beside me, whistling a broken tune. The ship heaved and we bumped up against each other and in the press of bodies, I felt his lingering touch. As seagulls wheeled and cried overhead and the ship groaned through the water, he gripped my hand and boldly pulled it to his crotch and then, just as sudden, let it go. I was surprised by this act of aggressive tenderness and wondered at the boy's fearlessness. He was about sixteen, I guessed, but couldn't be sure. I wanted to tell him that dropping the hand like that was a risky business.

'I'm Charlie,' I said. 'What's yours?'

He looked at me blankly as if he grasped nothing of my words. He must be a foreigner, I assumed, who didn't understand English.

'*Parlez-vous français?*' I chanced, which was my sum total of French.

He gave a strangled grunt and with his hand gestured to his ears and mouth to let me know that he was deaf and dumb. I was lost for words. A fraught silence enfolded us until I heard him sob as if all the heartache of his affliction had all of a sudden welled up in him. I didn't know what caused this outburst of crying but I threw my arms around him and drew him close. He hung on to me tightly and cried his eyes out. A silence, an unknowingness, surrounded him that made me sad. When a crowd of very drunk and boisterous men staggered towards where we were standing, he moved off at once and disappeared below deck. I stood there in the night, too distraught to move, thinking about the ordeal of his life. I could do nothing other than through poems, perhaps, to give tongue to the silence that strangled him.

A little later, I saw him asleep on a long seat, his head cradled in the lap of a matronly woman in a grey frock and bonnet who gazed at him fondly. I returned to my seat opposite the priest where I had deposited my luggage. He was lying back, his green bag lodged tightly behind his legs, a set of rosary beads entwined in his fingers. God looks after those who look after themselves. There we sat, a budding poet and an ageing priest engrossed in our own thoughts. I was trying to bring to mind something that Wallace Stevens said about poetry being a means of salvation when one loses faith in religion. Anyway, the poet and the priest perform similar roles. They are both mediators between the profane and the sacred, the temporal and the eternal.

Sitting there, mulling over my homecoming to parents, to a language and a place, I couldn't get 'Ithaca', a poem by Cavafy, out of my mind. *The Odyssey* is the epic story of Odysseus travelling back to Ithaca, his homeplace, after the siege of Troy. In the poem, Cavafy commends the voyage. Arriving at one's destination is nothing, it is the journey itself that is important, the adventures and the intoxications of it, the knowledge gleaned along the way; and finally, when one arrives in Ithaca, it may be disappointing but nevertheless, you have been strengthened and made wise by the voyage. Ithaca is not to be faulted, however dreary, tame and commonplace it is, it provided you with that voyage – your passage to maturity.

I was no longer a *'glas-stócach'*, a green unseasoned youth. I was twenty years old, a young adult embarked on a perilous but promising journey back to my own Ithaca.

NOTE ON THE AUTHOR

Cathal O'Searcaigh is one of the foremost poets writing in Gaelic, a member of Aos Dána and a recipient of many major awards including the *Irish Times* Literature Prize and the American Ireland Literary Fund. A native Gaelic speaker, he lives on his ancestral hill farm at the foot of Mount Errigal in County Donegal. His poems have been translated into numerous languages but *Light on Distant Hills* is his first work to be written in English.